To June, a God love-gift
to you ... y 2016!
Mu

Steve

Can God Guide
My Life?

Steve Kitt
MA, BA (Hons), PGCE, DipTEFLA

New Wine Press

New Wine Press

An imprint of
Roperpenberthy Publishing Ltd
Springfield House
23 Oatlands Drive
Weybridge KY13 9LZ
United Kingdom

ISBN 978-1-905991-97-6

Cover design Spiffingcovers
Cover photo by FionaMillsArt
Designed and typeset in the UK by **documen**,www.documen.co.uk
Printed in the United Kingdom

CONTENTS

ABOUT THE AUTHOR

Steve became a believer in July 1985. A BA (Hons) graduate, as well as the holder of a Master's Degree, he has worked for many years as a teacher of English as a foreign language. A speaker of both Spanish and Portuguese, he has also operated as an international missionary, starting with a Discipleship Training School with Youth With A Mission (YWAM) Jamaica in 1991, involving month-long trips to Trinidad and Curaçao. Subsequent callings have taken him to such diverse countries as Sweden, India, Vietnam and – his principal calling – South America, particularly Brazil (also Chile and Paraguay). He has ministered extensively to children, but also ministers to adults.

FOREWORD

This book will hopefully be beneficial to a range of people in their walk in life. It may be that you have recently come to faith and are now asking the question, "Now what? Where do I go from here?" Perhaps you have been a believer for many years and now wish to pass on your experience to others. If so, then my hope is that this book will serve as a teaching aid to you. Alternatively, you may be in a place in life where you are questioning whether there is a God at all. If this is the case, then I hope that this book can help you to come up with some answers which are satisfactory to you. Wherever you are in life, I wish you well in your journey.

Steve

Dedicated to Mum

Introduction

Can God guide my life?

"The Lord is my shepherd, I shall not be in want. He makes me lie down in green pastures, he leads me beside quiet waters, he restores my soul. He guides me in paths of righteousness for his name's sake. Even though I walk through the valley of the shadow of death, I will fear no evil, for you are with me; your rod and your staff they comfort me. You prepare a table for me in the presence of my enemies. You anoint my head with oil; my cup overflows. Surely goodness and love will follow me all the days of my life, and I will dwell in the house of the Lord forever."

Famous words from Psalm 23. The question is how does it work in practice? How does God shepherd me? How does God guide me? What part do I have to play, if any? Whilst acknowledging that God is mysterious and unfathomable, this book will attempt to show, practically, how these things may come about.

PART 1

Ways in which God can guide us

Taking a calculated step of faith

God's guiding hand, then and now

In Genesis 6 we read The Bible's account of a global flood,

> *"The Lord saw how great man's wickedness on the earth had become, and that every inclination of the thoughts of his heart was only evil all the time. The Lord was grieved that he had made man on the earth, and his heart was filled with pain. So the Lord said, 'I will wipe mankind, whom I have created, from the face of the earth.'"*
>
> (from verse 5)

We read that Noah was a righteous man, blameless among the people of his time, who walked with God. God – in great detail – instructed Noah to build an ark. God was then to send rain on the earth for 40 days and 40 nights to wipe from the face of the earth every living creature he had made, bar those that had made it onto the ark.

The earth – and Noah – had never seen rain before. But Noah had heard the voice of God clearly. Noah's task, therefore, was to take a calculated step of faith and to construct the ark, not knowing exactly how events would appear subsequently.

Abram (later Abraham) had a comparable situation, which we read about in Genesis 12,

> *"The Lord had said to Abram, 'Leave your country, your people and your father's household and go to the land I will show*

you. I will make you into a great nation and I will bless you; I will make your name great, and you will be a blessing.'"

(from verse 1)

As was the case with Noah, so it was with Abram; he had partial information. He, also, was required to take a calculated step of faith and start moving, not knowing where this would ultimately lead him. But he had heard the voice of God clearly.

I was in a similar situation in 2003. I was coming to the end of a very fruitful year at Bible College in Sweden. I was praying, and suddenly saw the vision of a flag – it was almost as if I were kneeling on top of the flag itself. I recognised the flag as the flag of Brazil – a country I had previously had no interest in. Whilst kneeling, I subsequently heard that *"still small voice"* (refer to 1 Kings 19:11-13) saying, "Keep it in mind for the future." As did Noah and Abram, I heard the voice of God clearly. God had plans for me in Brazil. As such, I needed to take a calculated step of faith; I started to learn Portuguese. Looking back, I can now see God's hand on my life from years previously; I had spent Autumn 1993 to Summer 1995 teaching English in Spain. This had been a difficult period in my life and, at the time, it certainly did not feel as if God was involved at all. I was struggling to learn Spanish and, as a consequence, was struggling socially. At that time, I worked very hard on the Spanish language. Now, a little over 10 years later, the Portuguese language (closely related to Spanish) came relatively easily to me as a result of that difficult period in the mid-90s. God can see far into the future, and we need to trust Him when we are in circumstances which are hard and, seemingly, unfruitful. There may be benefits later on if we persevere.

Can God speak to me through His Word, the Bible?

This has to be the first 'port of call' for a Christian. We have to believe that God has given us the Bible for our guidance. Psalm 119:105-106 states that,

> "Your word is a lamp to my feet and a light for my path. I have taken an oath and confirmed it, that I will follow your righteous laws."

And 2 Timothy 3:16 says,

> "All Scripture is God-breathed and is useful for teaching, rebuking, correcting and training in righteousness."

As such, any pictures, words, voices, etc, we feel we have received from God must be compatible with God's Word. If they are not, then ignore them.

Can God speak to me through pictures?

Yes, He can, but sometimes we need to seek a little. Matthew 7:7 tells us,

"Seek and you shall find."

In 1991, I was at a crossroads in my life. I was praying with a Christian friend and saw a vision of an aeroplane flying over tropical vegetation. It was very clear. I remember telling my friend that I thought God wanted me to travel. The next phase of the vision came later. I was going to Spain on holiday, and my initial thought was that maybe God wanted me there. However, after that trip, where I had sought – and failed – to spot vegetation similar to that of the vision, I returned home and concluded that this was not the intended location. A few days later, I received a word – almost as if it were written "in my spirit", 'JAMAICA'! And I knew, there and then. I handed in my notice at work and bought a 6-month return ticket, from September 1991 to March 1992.

When I got there, I had three closed doors in the first week. Bear in mind I was offering to do *voluntary* work! How can three groups of people turn down someone who just wanted to serve and was not seeking recompense? Doubts began to enter my mind; maybe I hadn't heard from God at all? Maybe this had all just been in my head? As I swam in a pool, thoughts came to me such as spending a month or two touring around Jamaica before returning to England. Perhaps a short time in the United States. I felt quite disheartened. Then I was introduced to two leaders of a group called YWAM (Youth With A Mission), and subsequently was invited to attend their Discipleship Training School (DTS). I had heard of YWAM, but had no idea they had a base in Jamaica. It turned out to be a fantastic experience and a time of great spiritual growth. I took one particular risk there – they wanted someone to preach during their outreach to Trinidad, and I offered – something I had never done before. I was nervous but God anointed it. No prizes for guessing when the DTS ran: September 1991 to March 1992! Absolutely amazing! Had I gone a month earlier, or a month later, it would have been unworkable, but God knew exactly when I needed to be there.

In July 2001 I visited Norway (a city called Bergen) for three weeks, taking in a trip to Sweden for a one-week Christian convention. About five people at the convention said to me, "You must come here to the Bible College." I prayed and God showed me a picture of a magnificent goose flying high in the sky – it was majestic. I negotiated with God (not normally advisable!) that if I saw a goose in the next two days (before returning to England), this would be confirmation for me that God wanted me to go to the Bible College. Despite being on constant watch, I saw nothing! Then, the morning I was due to fly home, I was in a park in Bergen and saw a group of pathetic geese that couldn't even fly walking round and round a small pen! I felt God say, "Steve, which of these geese do you want to be? Like these pathetic ones or like the magnificent one you saw in the vision?" I chose the magnificent one! I spent 13 months studying Swedish and went in August 2002 for nine fantastic months at Bible College.

Can God speak to me through a chain of events?

In 2005, round about April time, I had an incredible urge to phone my friend Jacqueline Pringle in America. She was from England and had moved to America a few years previously to attend Bible College. I had not spoken to her for about 2 years, and it was a strange time to be thinking about phoning her; 11 o'clock on a Thursday night, when I was working the next morning and would normally have been thinking about getting some sleep! After a general catch-up, she became very animated and asked me what I was doing over the weekend. A well-known North American preacher was in England, and Jacqueline was urging me to drive two-and-a-half hours from my home to attend his conference (don't forget, she didn't even know I was going to phone her!). As it was, I was finishing work that particular Friday at 1pm, so did, in fact, make the drive. On arrival there at about 4pm, I was surprised to see a previous pastor of mine, John France, who I hadn't seen for some 13 years. He pointed me in the direction of a group of guys from the same church who I hadn't seen over the same period. One of them, John Bennett, invited me for a burger. We got talking, and he invited me on a missions trip to India the following October. I said I would give it some thought, and we returned to the main evening meeting of the conference. The first thing they spoke about? Yes – missions trips to India! John had had no idea they would be doing this, so I signed up for his trip there and then! We went to India in October 2005, preaching, praying for the sick and witnessing many miracle healings, such as freedom from asthma, bronchitis, back problems and neck problems.

On one occasion in India, I was telling John about my Brazil vision. He knew a Brazilian woman called Miriam Pinheiro who was at that time living in England as a missionary. On returning to England, we were introduced, developed a friendship, and she was able to connect me with a church in Brazil. The church was Igreja Shalon in Curitiba, a city I had never heard of. Strangely, my close friend Dave Doyle also had a vision to visit Brazil. He was in contact with a girl there called Helga who he was planning to do ministry with. Her home city? Oh yes – it was Curitiba! Dave had never previously heard of this city, either. What a chain of events, and it all started one Thursday night when a thought came to me to phone Jacqueline in America. In case you are not sure, that thought was not my own – that was the Holy Spirit prompting me to make a phone call which would (very indirectly) change my life. On my first day in Brazil, Miriam introduced me to the pastor, Odilon Vergara. We connected immediately, and it was the start of many great adventures for me at Igreja Shalon. As I write, I have been to Brazil eight times, spending a total of about 8 months there, sharing my testimony, preaching (to both adults and children) and teaching English to church members.

Can God speak to me through other people?

Yes, absolutely He can, and it can often serve to clarify an otherwise confused situation.

In 2012, I had returned to Sweden to attend the second year of Bible College (actually a four month stint). During the course, all students were required to select a missions destination, which the Dean of the College would endeavour to place the student in, if workable. There were a number of possible countries on offer, including Sweden itself, Russia, Bulgaria, Estonia, India, Mongolia, China and Vietnam (possibly more).

I wrestled with the possibilities. The Asian countries appealed more, primarily because I considered that these were countries that had been the most unreached with the Gospel. I had already been to India, and did not feel drawn to Mongolia. That left China and Vietnam. Both countries had their appeal (and potential danger). If anything, I was leaning more in my mind towards China, although Proverbs 3:5 instructs us to trust in the Lord with all our hearts and not to lean on our own understanding. It was whilst out cycling in the Swedish countryside that a thought came to me. I decided to return home later on that day and ask a girl living in the house I was staying at (Michele Hand) to close her eyes, picture the world, imagine she was flying around it, and then stop before naming the country she had stopped at. On doing this, to my amazement she said, "Vietnam"! I had not previously discussed missions trips with her nor given the reason why I had asked her to do this. She could have named any country in the entire world – not just the ones I listed earlier on – but it was Vietnam that she named. Suddenly – through another person – it was clear; Vietnam would be my destination.

And what a fruitful trip it turned out to be. Firstly, due to my greater experience and (hopefully!) maturity, I was asked to lead the group which contained three Swedish guys in their early 20s as well as a Finnish man in his 50s. This was an opportunity for me to develop man-management skills which I wasn't even sure that I had! The trip also presented many Bible teaching and preaching opportunities (for all the group, although two members declined), as well as opportunities to pray for people in their various needs – physical and spiritual. We witnessed two miracle healings whilst there; a deaf man recovered his hearing, and a 12-year-old boy who had been sweating profusely in his hands and feet for over six months was completely healed. Both miracles occurred after we had prayed for them. And, again, in case you are wondering, that thought that had come to me to ask Michele to close her eyes, picture the world, imagine she was flying around it, and then stop before naming the country she had stopped at did not originate from me; it was, once again, the Holy Spirit. He knew exactly what answer Michele was going to give. In fact, maybe he popped the thought into Michele Himself!

On another occasion, I was at church meeting in Plymouth, England. The pastor there, Pastor John Smith, a very inspirational preacher from Northern Ireland, asked any members of the congregation who were going through a difficult time to stand up. At that time, I was going through a difficult situation, so I stood, along with about eight other people. He spoke words over all of us, individually. When he came to me, he said something like, "I don't know what you are going through, but the answer is in the post." He continued by saying that he didn't know why he had said that, but perhaps it would mean something to me. That very week, I received a letter inviting me to work in my home town of Bognor Regis. Pastor John's prophetic word had been spot-on!

Can God use me to help guide the lives of others?

Yes He can, and He will often use the gifts of the Spirit to do so. And it is worth stressing that we are to *"eagerly desire spiritual gifts"* as Paul urges us in 1 Corinthians 14:1. As such, it is worth taking time to examine these, and see how they operate. I will use a combination of examples from the Bible as well as from my own life to illustrate how they can work.

> *"There are different kinds of gifts, but the same Spirit. There are different kinds of service, but the same Lord. There are different kinds of working, but the same God works all of them in all men. Now to each one the manifestation of the Spirit is given for the common good. To one there is given through the Spirit the message of wisdom, to another the message of knowledge by means of the same Spirit, to another faith by the same Spirit, to another gifts of healing by that one Spirit, to another miraculous powers, to another prophecy, to another distinguishing between spirits, to another speaking in different kinds of tongues, and to still another the interpretation of tongues. All these are the work of one and the same Spirit, and he gives them to each one, just as he determines..."*
>
> (1 Corinthians 12:4-11)

The gift of wisdom is essentially the ability to know what to do or say in a particular situation. For example, we read of Stephen in Acts 6:10 that his accusers *"could not stand up against his wisdom or the Spirit by which he spoke"*.

The gift of knowledge is insight into a person or situation that would not be obvious to the naked eye. In Matthew 16:16 when Jesus has asked the disciples who they say He is, Peter immediately responded,

"You are the Christ, the Son of the living God," to which Jesus replied, *"Blessed are you, Simon son of Jonah, for this was not revealed to you by man, but by my Father in heaven."* In other words, it was a word of knowledge.

Regarding the gift of faith. Well, we all have faith, but this is referring to faith for a specific situation. Moses parting the Red Sea is a likely example.

Gifts of healing were illustrated from my trip to Vietnam where, in the name of Jesus, a deaf man received his hearing and a 12-year-old boy was healed of his profuse sweating.

The gift of miraculous powers. Perhaps Samson and his supernaturally-endowed strength would be an example?

The gift of prophecy, we are told in 1 Corinthians 14:3, is to speak to men *"for their strengthening, encouragement and comfort"*. Andy Elmes, my pastor in Portsmouth from 2004 to 2010, once prophesied over me that I would influence thousands. Technically, I achieved this in one day, when asked to give my testimony to some 2,500 Brazilians at Igreja Shalon (church) in Curitiba in March 2011, although I hope it didn't stop there!

The gift of discernment enables a believer to distinguish between true spirits and false spirits. For example, in Acts 16:18, Paul recognised in the slave girl that, despite her apparent glowing praises (*"These men are servants of the Most High God"*), she was being manipulated by an evil spirit, which he subsequently cast out of her.

The gift of tongues is, I believe, for all believers. Paul, in 1 Corinthians 14:5, states,

"I would like every one of you to speak in tongues."

It is a language given to a believer by the Holy Spirit. It may or may not be an earthly language, spoken by a particular people group. It has a range of possible functions. For example, in Acts 2:1-8 we are informed that tongues was used to speak to people in their own native tongue.

In my own life, I have been in a meeting (in Bognor Regis, England) where I was speaking in tongues. Unbeknown to me, a lady present – Meg Evans – knew German, and told me that I had been speaking in German and was able to tell me what I had been saying! An encouragement to me, but an even greater encouragement to Meg, as the word would have been specifically for her. On another occasion a church I was part of – Portsmouth Family Church in England – were having a men's "Advance" in Niton, on the Isle of Wight. On one occasion, the guys were singing in tongues and the pastor – Andy Elmes – was repeating over and over again "Sigue alabando, sigue alabando". One of the guys there was Miguel from Argentina, who was able to inform Andy that "Sigue alabando" means "Keep praising" in Spanish! Andy had never studied Spanish before.

1 Corinthians 14:4 tells us that *anyone who speaks in a tongue edifies himself.* We are also told in 1 Corinthians 14:22 that tongues *are a sign, not for believers but for unbelievers.* And in Ephesian 6, straight after Paul has instructed believers to put on the full armour of God, he then tells us (in verse 18): *and pray in the Spirit on all occasions with all kinds of prayers and requests. With this in mind, be alert and always keep on praying for all the saints.* I would take "pray in the Spirit" to mean "pray in tongues", and – given when he has said this – I believe it refers, at least in part, to spiritual warfare; waging war against unseen forces of wickedness. So tongues has a number of different functions.

The interpretation of tongues enables all believers to understand what was said in a tongue in a meeting. I have witnessed this happening on a number of occasions.

In my own life, I can give examples of how God has used me to guide the lives of others using spiritual gifts. In all the following examples, praying in tongues was involved. This is key. Another important thing is to declare what you believe God has shown you, either by way of picture, spoken or (in your spirit) written word. Even if it means nothing to you, it may well mean something to the other person.

In my early days as a believer, I recall two separate occasions when I received words of knowledge for other people. One was in a meeting of about fifty people in Bognor Regis, England, where I saw a picture of a rib cage opening and closing, as it would when breathing. I also got an impression – I think even a spoken word – that it was painful for the person in question to breathe in. On speaking out this vision, a middle-aged Irish gentleman named Victor acknowledged that he had received a severe blow to the ribcage. We were able to pray for him.

On the other occasion, in a similar-sized meeting (same location), I saw a picture of the bone structure of a person's foot. It was clear from the picture that a bone had been previously broken but had not aligned correctly when it knitted together again. On speaking out this picture, an elderly lady named Daphne declared that she had this problem and, again, we were able to pray for her.

In April 2012 in Curitiba (Brazil), I was in a small group meeting, praying in tongues. I saw a picture of a pair of hands in an x-ray form and felt the Holy Spirit say that a person in that room had some discomfort in that area. I spoke out what I had seen, and my friend Miriã Gisely Duarte Fernandes responded – she had repetitive strain injury, the type you get, for example, from excessive typing. We were able to pray for her. On another occasion in Curitiba, I had a picture of a lady's foot. Again, somebody responded and we were able to minister to her.

The above words of knowledge were fairly straightforward in their interpretation. However, on other occasions they were not – at least not to me. I was at a Bible weekend in Buxton, England, lying on my bed prior to Saturday breakfast and praying (in tongues). I saw the imprint of an animal's foot in the ground, and heard a voice stressing to me that it was a bear's footprint. I then saw a lady's shoe, which had a stiletto heel. I then saw the two together; the bear's footprint in front of the lady's shoe. During the first morning meeting, I noticed that the wife of the Bible teacher was wearing shoes like the one I had seen in the vision. After the meeting I spoke to her and she informed me that I would never have seen those shoes before. On telling her of my vision, she was taken aback. It turned out that her husband was a very hairy man and that – unbeknown to anyone else – she nicknamed him the bear! She had received words previously about interrupting her husband whilst he was teaching, and she knew that my vision was the latest addition! Of course I could have had no way of knowing what this vision meant – it was specific to her. I could name this couple, but perhaps I shouldn't!

On another occasion, a woman, Pat Tyacke – in her 70s at the time – came bounding up to me asking me if I remembered praying for her some 10 years previously. I told her that I did. She then asked me if I remembered receiving a picture for her. In fact she needed to remind me that I had received a picture of an old World War II aeroplane, known as a Spitfire. She then went on to inform me that this had changed her life! *A picture that I had received for her 10 years previously, that had meant nothing to me at all, had changed her life!* This reinforces what I mentioned earlier; if you think you have seen something in the Spirit when you are praying, make sure you give it out – even if it seems very obscure and means nothing to you at all. It could be the key to unlocking a door for another person. To reinforce this point further, I once when praying with a girl saw a vision of an instrument being played. On telling the girl, this was exactly what she needed to hear for her particular circumstances at that time; she saw herself as an instrument for God to play.

God once used me as part of a sequence of events. It was again in Buxton and we were in the Friday evening meeting. I received a vision of a canoe – the type you would see on the Amazon River, cut out from a large tree trunk. The canoe was wide enough to have two people sitting side by side, each holding a paddle. The river was perfectly calm and still and yet the canoe was rocking; the two people were totally out of sync with each other. I had no interpretation for this vision, but it was such a clear picture; I felt sure that I had heard from God and shared what I had seen with the group (there were about 14 of us). Nobody responded. I was disappointed as I really felt I had seen clearly. However, during the Saturday morning meeting, a South African man (I forget his name) stated that he had an interpretation for my vision. The two people in the canoe represented a married couple –both with us for that weekend – whose marriage was in trouble. The man went on to say that if the issues were not dealt with, the marriage would end. There was a period of silence in the room before a brave lady confessed that the vision was for her and her husband. From that moment on, the emphasis of the weekend changed, and this couple were able to receive ministry from the Bible teacher and his wife. The couple being ministered to were actually a pastor and his wife. On this occasion, God chose to use four people to reach this couple. I would imagine this would have been to encourage all six of us; I was encouraged to have received an accurate vision, the South African man would have been encouraged to receive an accurate interpretation, and the visiting Bible teacher and his wife were able to use their particular gifts to minister to the couple in question.

God also once spoke to me via a dream for a person! It was in July 2001, at the Swedish Christian Conference (the same week that I received the 'goose' vision). I woke up at what must have been sometime between about midnight and two o'clock in the morning having seen a clear picture of a girl. She had a Middle-Eastern look, a long straight nose and a distinctive hairstyle which wasn't unattractive but nonetheless made me think of an upturned bird's nest! I went back to sleep. I got up in the morning, and went off to the conference. The conference began. A short time after that (maybe 10 or 15 minutes?) a girl sat on the end of the row I was sitting on, holding a camcorder. *It was the very girl I had seen in my dream!*

The meeting finished, and I asked God what I should do. I felt Him say "Go and talk to her", which I did. As we talked, it was clear that she was a brand new Christian – maybe about a week old, spiritually speaking – and that morning she hadn't been at all motivated to attend the conference, but eventually decided to come (I suspect a prompting from the Holy Spirit!). She had been filming the event and had moved to my row to get a better view. If I remember rightly, she said that she'd come from Iran (although I think she used the term "Persia" – its previous name under a different regime). Her husband was also a recent convert – about one year previously. The rest of her family, and his family, were Moslem. As we continued to talk, in my mind I was praying (men *can* multi-task when they put their minds to it!). I felt God giving me a scripture to relate to her from Acts 16:31,

"Believe in the Lord Jesus, and you will be saved – you and your household."

She was greatly encouraged by this and the fact that God had given a complete stranger a dream about her! God was clearly interested in her as an individual; now she knew it. The following day I met her husband and little daughter, and there was a bond between us for the rest of that week.

I mentioned earlier in this section that I had the privilege of sharing my testimony (life story) in front of some 2,500 people at Igreja Shalon, Curitiba in March 2011. There was an interesting and unintended (on my part!) consequence to this, which I will relate to you. As part of my testimony, I shared the story of how God challenged me with the vision of a high-flying goose. As I was coming to a close, I challenged the people by saying (in my very best Portuguese!), "Don't be a pathetic goose: FLY!...FLY!...FLY!" I found out some time later that a lady there had taken these words very literally; up until that point, she had had a fear of flying (aerophobia). As I was speaking, God was speaking to her regarding this phobia, and she subsequently went out and bought a flight ticket. She took the flight, and the phobia was gone. Praise God!

What is Baptism in the Holy Spirit?

This is worth examining in the light of the previous section. It is an expression which is used commonly in church circles, and opinion is divided as to what it actually means. It is a term to describe a movement of the Holy Spirit upon / in a believer. There is further division among Christians regarding *when* it occurs. Does it occur at salvation or does it occur some time after salvation? Or will it vary from person to person? Returning to Acts 2 and the Day of Pentecost, *all were filled with the Holy Spirit and began to speak in other tongues as the Spirit enabled them*. Presuming that this is an example of the baptism of the Holy Spirit then it is clear that in this case it has occurred *after* salvation; these were the disciples who had been walking with Jesus for at least three years. There is a further example to support this in the Book of Acts in Chapter 19:1-6,

> "He [Paul] *found some disciples and asked them, 'Did you receive the Holy Spirit when you believed?' They answered, 'No, we have not even heard that there is a Holy Spirit.' So Paul asked, 'Then what baptism did you receive?' ' John's baptism,' they replied. Paul said, 'John's baptism was a baptism of repentance. He told the people to believe in the one coming after him, that is, in Jesus.' On hearing this, they were baptised into the name of the Lord Jesus. When Paul placed his hands on them, the Holy Spirit came on them, and they spoke in tongues and prophesied.*"

In my own life, the sequence was as follows: I repented of my sins and received Jesus Christ as my Lord and Saviour in July, 1985. At that moment, the Holy Spirit came to live in me. Ephesians 1:13 states,

"And you also were included in Christ when you heard the word of truth, the gospel of your salvation. Having believed, you were marked in him with a seal, the promised Holy Spirit, who is a deposit, guaranteeing our inheritance."

In November 1987, I was invited to a Pentecostal church in Plymouth, England. Here, a lot of people were singing in tongues, something which I had never heard of up until that point. The Holy Spirit fell upon me in a very dramatic fashion; very real, very tangible and very powerful. It is something that I find very difficult to put into words – like having a shower on the inside is as good a description as any. This, without doubt, transformed my life; things were never the same again. This was me being baptised in the Holy Spirit, over two years after my salvation. And let me reiterate: this was not an experience I had been seeking after; it was something which simply happened to me at God's discretion and in God's timing.

A few months after that, in February 1988, I spent a week in Oxford, England, to attend an accountancy course (a profession I was trying to succeed in at that time!). There, I encountered David Gordon, who I vaguely knew from my schooldays in Bognor Regis (he had been the year below me at school). On conversing, it became clear that we were both Christians, he a more mature one than I. As our friendship developed, he asked me if I spoke in tongues to which I replied that I did not but would like to. So, one day we sat down together and made this our goal. I didn't know how to start, so he told me that he would pray in tongues, and that I should start making utterances; it might well be me to begin with, but the Holy Spirit would take over and it would begin to flow. And that is exactly how it turned out. After that, I prayed in tongues every day; it was so exciting. That's how things went for me, but that is not to say that it wouldn't be a different sequence of events for other believers. I was baptised in water in September, 1988.

Water Baptism

So how important is water baptism, then? Is it something that we need to do, and are there consequences if we don't? Personally, I have met people who clearly have a Christian belief but have told me that they never hear anything from God. They also sometimes say that they never 'feel' anything, but we need to be careful here; Christianity is a faith, not a feeling. Having said that, God has designed us to have feelings and they should not be ignored altogether. One thing many of these people have had in common is this: they have not been water baptised. This might be the key for them.

Baptism is so much more than merely a symbol. When we are saved, we are spiritually baptized into Christ (Galatians 3:27,) and into His Body, the church (1 Corinthians 12:13). Baptism in water is an outward representation of these inward realities. In Biblical symbolism, water represents inner cleansing (Ephesians 5:26, Hebrews 10:22,) and spiritual rebirth (John 3:5,) both of which are central themes of baptism. Water baptism is, in essence, a funeral. It is an act of faith in which we testify, both to God and to the world, that the person we were before is dead and buried, and we are raised as a new creation in Christ. This is beautifully illustrated by these Scriptures,

"We were therefore buried with him through baptism into death in order that, just as Christ was raised from the dead through the glory of the Father, we too may live a new life."

(Romans 6:4)

"having been buried with him in baptism and raised with him through your faith in the power of God, who raised him from the dead."

(Colossians 2:12)

When someone is properly baptized they are wholly immersed in water, not just sprinkled. This is why the above verse in Romans says we are "buried" with Him in baptism. To go down into what could be called "The Watery Grave" is to identify with the death and burial of Jesus Christ on our behalf. It's actually a way of saying, "I died to my own sinful self when I gave my life to Jesus." Second, to rise up out of the watery grave is a way of identifying with the resurrection of Jesus Christ from the dead. It's actually a way of saying, "I've been raised from my former dead life of sin and have risen to a new life in Jesus." So, it's easy to see that Water Baptism is simply an outward expression of an inward experience. It's the Born Again Believer's way of saying, "I completely identify with the death, burial and resurrection of Jesus Christ on my behalf." This is why it is not Biblical or acceptable to "sprinkle" baptize an infant. Infants are unable to identify with the death, burial and resurrection of Jesus. Their undeveloped little minds cannot possibly comprehend such a thing.

Being baptized is a command from God, not an option. It is an act that God requires of every believer. In fact, among Jesus' last recorded words on earth were,

> "He that believes and is baptized shall be saved..."
>
> (Mark 16:16)

Think about that for a moment. Jesus' very call to believe on Him includes a call to be baptized. If He puts it in that category, He must see it as being something very important, wouldn't you say? You never read of an unbaptized Christian anywhere in the Bible. In fact, baptism immediately followed a person's salvation. They didn't see it as something to be delayed or put off. Let's take a look at some of the conversions described in the Book of Acts.

When the people respond to Peter's sermon on the Day of Pentecost, the first thing he instructs them to do is,

> "Repent, and be baptized every one of you in the name of Jesus Christ for the forgiveness of your sins, and you will receive the gift of the Holy Spirit."
>
> (Acts 2:38)

We further read in verse 41 that *those who accepted his message were baptized...*"

Acts 8:26-40 is the account of Phillip leading the Ethiopian eunuch to Christ. As they finish their discussion, the eunuch enthusiastically asks, *"What is hindering me from being baptized?"* to which Philip replies *"If you believe with all your heart, you may."* Then they come to a body of water, and Philip promptly baptizes him.

> *The first thing the apostle Paul was told to do after his conversion was to be baptized.*
>
> (Acts 22:16)

There are a number of other instances we could look at as well (Acts 10:46-48; 16:14-15; 16:33; 18:8; 19:1-5). In each of these cases, notice the sense of urgency that is attached to baptism. These people all responded to Jesus in simple faith. However, they didn't see their faith as complete until they had obeyed God by being baptized. Keep in mind that *faith without works* (corresponding actions) *is dead* (James 2:17). A living faith produces an obedient heart (Matthew 7:21; Luke 6:46; 1 John 2:3-4) and water baptism is to be our first act of obedience.

Christians who do not follow Jesus in water baptism have a much higher rate of backsliding than those who do. After all, if our walk with God didn't begin with the most basic act of obedience, it got off to a faulty foundation in the first place. This will make it more difficult to walk obediently in other areas of our lives. Baptism is a very special way of God communicating His love to us. When we receive God's saving grace, it is no accident that He calls us to identify with Him in a way that makes it real to us. Are you struggling with guilt over your past? It may be because you haven't yet given the person you once were a proper burial! Water baptism is a very powerful reminder of God's wonderful grace. The person we were before is dead forever, and we are raised with Jesus as a totally new creation,

> *"Therefore, if anyone is in Christ he is a new creation; the old has gone, the new has come!"*
>
> (2 Corinthians 5:17)

So what comes first, Baptism in the Holy Spirit or baptism in water? Actually in the Book of Acts, you will find examples of both. In my own case, I was baptised in the Holy Spirit first – in November 1987 – and later baptised in water (September 1988). But we certainly want and – I would suggest – need both. As you can see, you have absolutely nothing to lose, and everything to gain by following Jesus in water baptism. Ultimately, it all goes back to Jesus' statement in John 14:15.

"If you love me, keep my commandments."

Baptism is a simple, but profound act of obedience that you will carry with you for the rest of your life. If you have not yet taken this step, I strongly encourage you to do so as soon as possible.

God's guiding hand (using mature believers)

Lessons from Ruth

I now want to do a case study on a character from the Bible who God clearly guided, to see what lessons we can learn. That person was Ruth. Before analysing the story, there are a number of characters and places we will look at which represent people or places in our lives,

Ruth represents...me. Or you. Making correct decisions in life.

Orpah possibly represents...me! Or you. Making very bad decisions in life.

Naomi represents a mature Christian in your life who will guide you in the right direction. It is possibly a pastor, a cell leader, or a close Christian friend who is wise and mature.

Boaz the Redeemer represents a 'type' of Jesus Christ the Redeemer (for all of us).

Moab represents a place in life that God does NOT want you to be. It might be a geographical place, or it might be an area of your life such as your world of alcoholism, your world of drug addiction, your world of pornography (etcetera).

Israel represents a place in life where God DOES want you to be.

The servant girls represent servants of God (Christians).

"In the days when the judges ruled, there was a famine in the land, and a man from Bethlehem in Judah, together with his wife and two sons, went to live for a while in the country of Moab. The man's name was Elimelech, his wife's name Naomi, and the names of his two sons were Mahlon and Kilion. They were Ephrathites from Bethlehem, Judah. And they went to

Moab and lived there. Now Elimelech, Naomi's husband, died, and she was left with her two sons. They married Moabite women, one named Orpah and the other Ruth. After they had lived there about ten years, both Mahlon and Kilion also died, and Naomi was left without her two sons and her husband."

(Chapter 1, verses 1-5)

This is an example of a person who definitely did not listen to God or allow Him to guide him and his family. Elimelech was going through a difficult time, so he went to live in the country of Moab. This was a bad Idea. A better idea would have been for him to pray, trust God to provide for him, and stay in the promised land: Israel. In Moab, he died. And so did his sons. So, lesson number 1: If you are going through a difficult time...don't go to Moab! Don't go to your world of alcohol, drugs or pornography. Stay in the church, pray to God. Trust Him to take you through the difficult situation.

In fact, as we read verse 6, we see that God HAD provided food in Israel. God is faithful. Elimelech made a terrible mistake!

"When she heard in Moab that the Lord had come to the aid of His people by providing food for them, Naomi and her daughters-in-law prepared to return home from there. With her two daughters-in-law she left the place where she had been living and set out on the road that would take them back to the land of Judah. Then Naomi said to her two daughters-in-law, 'Go back, each of you, to you mother's home. May the Lord show kindness to you, as you have shown to your dead and to me. May the Lord grant that each of you will find rest in the home of another husband.' Then she kissed them and they wept aloud and said to her, 'We will go back with you to your people'. But Naomi said, 'Return home, my daughters. Why would you come with me? Am I going to have any more sons, who could become your husbands? Return home, my daughters; I am too old to have another husband. Even if I thought there was still hope for me – even if I had a husband tonight and then gave birth to sons – would you wait until they grew up? Would you remain unmarried for them? No, my daughters. It is more bitter

*for me than for you, because the Lord's hand has gone out
against me.'"*

(Chapter 1, verses 6-13)

We see that Naomi has made a good decision, after the terrible decision
her husband made – she is returning to Israel. Now the two daughters-
in-law also need to make a decision.

*"At this they wept again. Then Orpah kissed her mother-in-
law goodbye, but Ruth clung to her. 'Look', said Naomi, 'your
sister-in-law is going back to her people and her gods. Go
back with her.' But Ruth replied, 'Don't urge me to leave you
or to turn back from you. Where you go I will go, and where
you stay I will stay. Your people will be my people and your
God my God. Where you die, I will die, and there I will be
buried. May the Lord deal with me, be it ever so severely,
if anything but death separates you and me'. When Naomi
realised that Ruth was determined to go with her, she stopped
urging her."*

(Chapter 1, verses 14-18)

Orpah went back to Moab – probably a bad decision. Ruth chose to
go with Naomi to Israel – the right decision, as we will see later. So...
make your choice! Moab or Israel? Ruth, then, is now the equivalent
of a 'baby Christian'. Such a person needs guidance and nurturing.
Naomi was such a person; someone who had known God for some
time and who was in a position to be able to use her maturity and
wisdom considerably to help the younger believer.

*"So the two women went on until they came to Bethlehem.
When they arrived in Bethlehem, the whole town was stirred
because of them, and the women exclaimed, 'Can this be
Naomi?' Don't call me Naomi [pleasant],' she told them. 'Call
me Mara [bitter], because the Almighty has made my life very
bitter. I went away full, but the Lord has brought me back empty.
Why call me Naomi? The Lord has afflicted me; the Almighty
has brought misfortune upon me.' So Naomi returned from*

Moab accompanied by Ruth the Moabitess, her daughter-in-law, arriving in Bethlehem as the barley harvest was beginning."

(Chapter 1, verses 19-22)

When people return to the church who have been away, let's receive them with love and not an attitude of judgement.

And let's not forget there is a harvest to gather.

"Now Naomi had a relative on her husband's side, from the clan of Elimelech, a man of standing, whose name was Boaz. And Ruth the Moabitess said to Naomi, 'Let me go to the fields and pick up the leftover grain behind anyone in whose eyes I have found favour.' Naomi said to her, 'Go ahead, my daughter.' So she went out and began to glean in the fields behind the harvesters. As it turned out, she found herself working in a field belonging to Boaz, who was from the clan of Elimelech. Just then Boaz arrived from Bethlehem and greeted the harvesters, 'The Lord be with you!' 'The Lord bless you!' they called back. Boaz asked the foreman of his harvesters, 'Whose young woman is that?' The foreman replied, 'She is the Moabitess who came back from Moab with Naomi.' She said, 'Please let me glean and gather among the sheaves behind the harvesters.' She went into the field and has worked steadily from morning until now, except for a short rest in the shelter. So Boaz said to Ruth, 'My daughter, listen to me. Don't go and glean in another field and don't go away from here. Stay with my servant girls. Watch the field where the men are harvesting, and follow along after the girls. I have told the men not to touch you. And whenever you are thirsty, go and get a drink from the water jars the men have filled.'"

(Chapter 2, verses 1-9:)

Ruth is serving Boaz, and we see his protection over her life. We also see an instruction from him to stay with the servant girls and not to work in another field. Once again, we see an example of how a new believer should be under the guidance and protection of older, wiser believers. We are serving Jesus and are enjoying the favour of His protection. We also need to work with other Christians and not work outside of God's will for our lives.

> *"At this, she bowed down with her face to the ground. She exclaimed, 'Why have I found such favour in your eyes that you notice me – a foreigner?' Boaz replied, 'I've been told all about what you have done for your mother-in-law since the death of your husband – how you left your father and mother and your homeland and came to live with a people you did not know before. May the Lord repay you for what you have done. May you be richly rewarded by the Lord, the God of Israel, under whose wings you have come to take refuge.'"*
>
> (Chapter 2, verses 10-12)

We don't deserve God's mercy, but we have it!

> *"'May I continue to find favour in your eyes, my lord,' she said. 'You have given me comfort and have spoken kindly to your servant – though I do not have the standing of one of your servant girls.' At mealtime Boaz said to her, 'Come over here. Have some bread and dip it in the wine vinegar.' When she sat down with the harvesters, he offered her some roasted grain. She ate all she wanted and had some left over.'"*
>
> (Chapter 2, verses 13-14)

We are very much family in the eyes of God.

> *"As she got up to glean, Boaz gave orders to his men, 'Even if she gathers among the sheaves, don't embarrass her. Rather, pull out some stalks for her from the bundles and leave them for her to pick up, and don't rebuke her.' So Ruth gleaned in the field until evening. Then she threshed the barley she had gathered, and it amounted to about 22 litres. She carried it back to town, and her mother-in-law saw how much she had gathered. Ruth also brought out and gave her what she had left over after she had eaten enough. Her mother-in-law asked her, 'Where did you glean today? Where did you work? Blessed*

be the man who took notice of you!' Then Ruth told her mother-in-law about the one at whose place she had been working.'"

(Chapter 2, verses 15-19)

Ruth thought she had a small ministry (verse 2), but as we read verses 15-19 we discover that Boaz had bigger plans for her! It's the same for us – I have discovered in my life that God had much bigger plans for me than I could ever have imagined. I'm sure it's the same for you. Don't limit what God wants to do in your life!

"'The Lord bless him!' Naomi said to her daughter-in-law. 'He has not stopped showing his kindness to the living and the dead.' She added, 'That man is our close relative; he is one of our kinsman redeemers.'"

(Chapter 2, Verse 20)

Jesus is our Redeemer...and a close relative! We're the family of God! Fantastic!

"Then Ruth the Moabitess said, 'He even said to me, "stay with my workers until they finish harvesting all my grain."' Naomi said to Ruth her daughter-in-law, 'It will be good for you, my daughter, to go with his girls, because in someone else's field you might be harmed.' So Ruth stayed close to the servant girls of Boaz to glean until the barley and wheat harvests were finished."

(Chapter 2, verses 21-23)

There's a job to be done – we need to be harvesting, and don't stop until the day you die or Jesus returns! But there's that warning again... stay together. If you go outside of God's will for your life you might be harmed. Satan wants to destroy you.

In Chapter 4 verse 13 we see that there is a very happy ending as Boaz marries Ruth. If we read Matthew 1, verse 5, we see that Ruth is in the line of Jesus Christ. What a fantastic decision she made to go to Israel! Let's also make good decisions in life.

And let's not forget that one day we will all be part of the Bride at the biggest wedding of them all!!!

God will guide; God will provide

We have established by now that God does, indeed, want to guide your life. There is an implication in this that whatever He calls you to do in life (i.e. wherever He guides you), He will be your provider. As such, I feel at this point that it is worth examining the question of prosperity. Christians around the world disagree about the whole concept of prosperity. I want to look at prosperity from three perspectives:

◊   what is prosperity?
◊   is prosperity for every Christian?
◊   what do we do with our prosperity?

Let's examine the Word of God and see what the Bible actually says about prosperity.

First of all, God makes certain promises about our basic needs; He promises that He will always feed us and He will always clothe us. It's everywhere in the Bible, but we can look at just one scripture to confirm that what I'm saying is true!

"Therefore I tell you, do not worry about your life, what you will eat or drink; or about your body, what you will wear. Is not life more important than food, and the body more important than clothes? Look at the birds of the air; they do not sow or reap or store away in barns, and yet your heavenly Father feeds them. Are you not much more valuable than they? Who of you by worrying can add a single hour to his life? And why do you worry about clothes? See how the lilies of the field grow. They do not labour or spin. Yet I tell you that not even Solomon in all his splendour was dressed like one of these. If that is how God clothes the grass of the field, which is here today and tomorrow is thrown into the fire, will He not much more clothe you, o you of little faith? So do not

worry, saying 'What shall we eat?' or 'What shall we drink?' For the pagans run after all these things, and your heavenly Father knows that you need them. But seek first His kingdom and His righteousness, and all these things will be given to you as well. Therefore do not worry about tomorrow, for tomorrow will worry about itself. Each day has enough trouble of its own."

(Matthew 6.25-34)

So the Bible promises that God is going to feed us and clothe us...we don't need to ever worry about that.

But there's more! God wants us to have enough for ourselves and enough to give away! I believe that we are called to tithe – to give 10 percent of our income to God. That tells me that God promises to feed and clothe us with a maximum of 90 percent of our income. In the Body of Christ, opinion is, again, divided on the issue of tithing. Many believers consider that it was part of the old Jewish law and no longer applies to us. However, Abraham tithed long before the Jewish law came into being (see Genesis 14:18-20). Also in Malachi 3:8-12 we have both a rebuke and an amazing promise from God in relation to tithing,

"'Will a man rob God? Yet you rob me.' But you ask, 'How do we rob you?' 'In tithes and offerings. You are under a curse – the whole nation of you – because you are robbing me. Bring the whole tithe into the storehouse, that there may be food in my house. Test me in this,' says the Lord Almighty, 'and see if I will not throw open the floodgates of heaven and pour out so much blessing that you will not have room enough for it. I will prevent pests from devouring your crops, and the vines in your fields will not cast their fruit,' says the Lord Almighty. 'Then all the nations will call you blessed, for yours will be a delightful land,' says the Lord Almighty."

And there's more! We have already examined Psalm 23, but let's briefly return there. In verse 1 we read that the Lord is our Shepherd; we won't be in want. So – again – there's that promise of provision. Verse 5 says, *"my cup overflows."* In other words, God is going to give us more than we need. In verse 6 we are told that, *"surely goodness and love will follow me all the days of my life."* I don't speak the language of the original text, but I have been told that the word "follow" here is a very strong word which basically means that goodness and love are going to "run after" me all the days of my life; I can't escape them!

The term "prosperity" I believe refers to more than just money, although I think money is part of it. I think "prosperity" also refers to a rich family life, a rich social life, varied and interesting experiences (etcetera).

The Bible says in 3 John 2,

> *"I pray that you may prosper in all things and be in health, just as your soul prospers."*

So...next question: is prosperity for every Christian? Let's stay in the Psalms to answer this. Firstly, Psalm 35.27 tells us that,

> *"The Lord delights in the prosperity of His people."*

Psalm 128 says,

> *"Blessed are all who fear the Lord and walk in His ways. You will eat the fruit of your labour; blessings and prosperity will be yours."*

So...does it say "Blessed are a few"? "Blessed are some"? No – it says ALL! Perhaps there is a condition, though...to fear the Lord and walk in His ways. But let me repeat: prosperity is for EVERY believer.

What other promises do we have? Psalm 41 says,

> *"Blessed is he who cares about the weak; the Lord delivers him in times of trouble. The Lord will protect him and preserve his life; He will bless him in the land and not surrender him to his enemies. The Lord will sustain him on his sick bed and restore him from his bed of illness."*

A lot of promises here, but where does it start? That we care about the weak. Another condition, perhaps.

> *"Blessed is the man who does not walk in the counsel of the wicked nor stand in the way of sinners or sit in the seat of mockers. But his delight is in the Law of the Lord, and on His Law he meditates day and night. He is like a tree planted by streams of water, which yields its fruit in season and whose leaf does not wither. Whatever he does prospers."*
>
> (Psalm 1)

Whatever he does prospers!!! What a promise!!!

But – again – there is a condition...the man who meditates day and night on God's Word.

So...based on what we have just read, my advice to you is:

◊   fear the Lord and walk in His ways
◊   care about the weak
◊   meditate day and night on God's Word

...prosperity MUST follow! For EVERY believer (without exception).

So finally...what do we do with our prosperity? We use it wisely! Prosperity for me is not big houses and big cars. Prosperity for me is a rich and full LIFE. The Bible tells us in Matthew 6:19-20 not to lay up for ourselves earthly treasures, but Heavenly treasures. Share your prosperity with others. The Bible says,

> *"it is more blessed to give than to receive."*
>
> (Acts 20.35)

It also says in Proverbs 11.25 that,

> *"A generous man will prosper; he who refreshes others will himself be refreshed."*

Remember, Jesus said in Matthew 10.8,

> *"Freely you have received, freely give."*

PART 2

Difficulties along the way

What stops you flying?

In this book, we have already discussed a vision related to a high-flying goose! I believe it is God's will for all of His people to be like this goose; to prosper in life as He guides us. I hope that nobody reading this book wants to live life like the geese in that sad pen with their wings clipped! We don't want to **'talk'** an expansive life – we want to **live** one! It seems appropriate at this point, therefore, to examine possible reasons why some of us are not flying in life.

Are there any areas of our lives which are not submitted to God? These are the very areas that the devil will be looking to exploit. Putting it another way...what things in your life stop you flying? Throughout the Bible, there are characters who had maybe one weakness (which, in many cases, proved to be their downfall). How seriously do you take your promises? Can people trust your words? If you say you will do something, will you do it? In Matthew 21 verse 28 we read about a man who had two sons. He asked one son to help him in the vineyard. The son said he would go, but he didn't go. He then asked the second son, who said he didn't want to help, but later he repented and went to help. It is the second son who did the will of the father. In England, we have an expression: "Talk is cheap". Your words are important – if you say you are going to do something, please do it! If you are not sure if you can do something....don't make the promise! It's simple!

Samson

Samson was a mighty man of God, but his romancing of attractive, but ungodly, members of the opposite sex proved his downfall (refer to Judges Chapters 13-16). We are also informed in Judges 16:1 that he spent a night with a prostitute, which would strongly suggest that he had a problem with lust. We have much to learn from the story of Samson, but particularly the issue of choice of wife (or husband). The Bible tells us in 2 Corinthians 6:14-18,

> *"Do not be yoked together with unbelievers. For what do righteousness and wickedness have in common? Or what fellowship can light have with darkness? What harmony is there between Christ and Belial? Or what does a believer have in common with an unbeliever? What agreement is there between the temple of God and idols? For we are the temple of the living God. As God has said: 'I will live with them and walk among them, and I will be their God, and they will be my people.' Therefore, 'Come out from them and be separate,' says the Lord. 'Touch no unclean thing, and I will receive you.' And, 'I will be a Father to you, and you will be my sons and daughters,' says the Lord Almighty."*

These are strong words. You are either born-again and translated from the kingdom of darkness into the Kingdom of Light or you are not. There is no 'in-between' state, no fence for you to sit on. You are either 'in' or you are 'out'. Your choice of partner is the second most important decision you will ever have to make in your entire life. Readers of this book will fall into one of two categories; either you are married or you are single. If you are reading this and are married, then please love your wife (or husband) whether they are Christians or non-Christians. However, if you are single, then you still have this decision up ahead of you. Please don't shoot the messenger, but I would have to say that the Word of God is very clear on this; marry a fellow Christian.

On countless occasions I have witnessed Christians dating non-Christians. They generally do so with the best will in the world; they believe their partner will 'come round' to ultimately being a Christian. I hear expressions like "He's very interested" or "She's quite close to becoming a Christian". Quite close, maybe – but she isn't one. It might even be that your partner will attend church with you – with the motive of keeping you happy, and nothing more. When you're not around, they don't go to church. When you're not around, they have no interest in the Bible. Only when you're there, trying to encourage them to come to faith. And, all the time, you are romantically involved.

Of course there are occasions when it has a happy ending and the non-believing partner comes to faith. However, I have seen many more situations where they don't come to faith and the Christian loses their spiritual fervour, often quite significantly. To use an analogy; if one person is on a table and another is sitting on the floor by the table, it is much easier for the latter to pull the former off the table than for the former to drag the latter onto the table. Can you serve the Kingdom of God effectively whilst married to someone who perhaps doesn't even believe that there *is* a Kingdom of God? As I write all this, I am very aware of the fact that I have some very dear friends – three female friends are on my mind right now – who are married to non-believers. I hope and I pray that your marriages will be long and happy, and that your husband / wife will accept Jesus Christ.

David

David was alone one night when he spotted a beautiful woman bathing (2 Samuel 11). His next move should have been to avert his eyes, but sadly he failed to do this. He sent someone to find out about her and was informed that she was the wife of Uriah, who was on the battlefield at the time. End of story, you would hope. But sadly, no. He decided he wanted her, right there, right then, in a moment of lust. How complicit the woman (Bathsheba) was we don't know – it would not be easy to refuse a king. She became pregnant, which left David with a problem; he needed to cover his tracks. He recalled Uriah from the battlefield and instructed him to go to his house. Uriah was a man of great honour, and chose not to do so out of respect for his fellow soldiers. This perhaps would have cut David to the heart as it is likely that he himself should have been on the battlefield, as this was the *time when kings go off to war* (see verse 1). Uriah repeated his honourable act (or did he suspect something?) the following night before returning to battle. At this, David gave orders for him to be placed *in the front line where the fighting is fiercest. Then withdraw from him so he will be struck down and die* (see verse 15).

In other words, David tried to cover one sin (adultery) with another sin (murder). We must never do this! When we sin (and we do all the time), we need to come before God in repentance, ask for forgiveness and start again. No cover-ups. *Do not be deceived: God cannot be mocked. A man reaps what he sows. Whoever sows to please their flesh, from the flesh will reap destruction,* as we are told in Galatians 6:7-8. Confession is the only solution. 1 John 1:9 tells us that *If we confess our sins, he is faithful and just and will forgive us our sins and purify us from all unrighteousness.*

Peter

Peter's fear of what man might do to him caused him to deny any association at all with Jesus (Matthew 26:69-75). I sympathise with Peter. In his situation, it is quite possible that I would have done exactly the same thing. How about you? In fact, only emboldening by the Holy Spirit would enable me to do otherwise. And this is the key. We are warned of terrible times up ahead for Christians, suffering at the hands of the ungodly before Jesus Christ returns in power and glory. Jesus Himself warned us,

> *"Then you will be handed over to be persecuted and put to death, and you will be hated by all nations because of me. At that time many will turn away from the faith and will betray and hate each other."*

> (Matthew 24:9-10)

And in Mark 13:9 Jesus says,

> *"You must be on your guard. You will be handed over to the local councils and flogged in the synagogues. On account of me you will stand before governors and kings as witnesses to them."*

Strong words indeed. But it is inevitable. And of course we know that even today, there are Christians suffering greatly for their faith, particularly in Islamic or communist countries. Thankfully, we are not alone and will not be alone. Jesus also said,

> *"And surely, I am with you always, to the very end of the age"*

> (Matthew 28:20)

And for the moment of persecution, we are also instructed,

> *"When you are brought before synagogues, rulers and authorities, do not worry about how you will defend yourselves or what you will say, for the Holy Spirit will teach you at that time what you should say."*

(Luke 12:11-12)

Joseph

Joseph's boasting that his family would bow down before him (Genesis 37:6-9) further aggravated the jealousy his brothers already had for him, leading them to take action against him (Genesis 37:12-28). We must guard against boasting. I Corinthians 13:4 says: *it* [love] *does not boast.* And 1 John 2:16 informs us,

> *"For everything in the world – the cravings of sinful man, the lust of his eyes and the boasting of what he has and does – comes not from the Father but from the world."*

Jealousy, also, is a dangerous emotion. It is listed in Galatians 5:19-21 as one of the 'acts of the sinful nature',

> *"The acts of the sinful nature are obvious: sexual immorality, impurity and debauchery; idolatry and witchcraft; hatred, discord, jealousy, fits of rage, selfish ambition, dissensions, factions and envy; drunkenness, orgies, and the like. I warn you, as I did before, that those who live like this will not inherit the kingdom of God."*

Sin destroys, and jealousy can be part of this destruction.

Lot

Lot was the nephew of Abram, who accompanied him on his journey. Both of them prospered greatly, to such an extent that *their possessions were so great that they were not able to stay together.*

And quarrelling arose between Abram's herdsmen and the herdsmen of Lot (Genesis 13:6-7). Abram therefore suggested that the two groups part company, and gave Lot first choice of direction to pursue (verse 9). Lot chose the well watered Plain of Jordan (verse 11), and ultimately found himself in a wicked city known as Sodom (verse 12). His selfish ambition led him to compromise with the world, causing him to be *'tormented in his righteous soul by the lawless deeds he saw and heard'* (2 Peter 2.8). Sometimes what we see with our naked eye is not always the best option!

Judas

Judas' love of money proved too much of a temptation for him, leading to both stealing and betrayal. We learn in John 12:3-6 that he was a thief before the story of his betrayal,

> *"Then Mary took about a pint of pure nard, an expensive perfume; she poured it on Jesus' feet and wiped his feet with her hair. And the house was filled with the fragrance of the perfume. But one of his disciples, Judas Iscariot, who was later to betray him, objected, 'Why wasn't this perfume sold and the money given to the poor? It was worth a year's wages.' He did not say this because he cared about the poor but because he was a thief; as keeper of the money bag, he used to help himself to what was put into it."*

In a similar vein, we read about Ananias and Sapphira in Acts 5:1-11. They actually resorted to lying to the Holy Spirit to try to cover up their lack of integrity,

> *"Now a man named Ananias, together with his wife Sapphira, also sold a piece of property. With his wife's full knowledge he kept back part of the money for himself, but brought the rest and put it at the apostles' feet. Then Peter said, 'Ananias, how is it that Satan has so filled your heart that you have lied to the Holy Spirit and have kept for yourself some of the money you received for the land? Didn't it belong to you before it was*

sold? And after it was sold, wasn't the money at your disposal? What made you think of doing such a thing? You have not lied just to human beings but to God.' When Ananias heard this, he fell down and died. And great fear seized all who heard what had happened. Then some young men came forward, wrapped up his body, and carried him out and buried him. About three hours later his wife came in, not knowing what had happened. Peter asked her, 'Tell me, is this the price you and Ananias got for the land?' 'Yes,' she said, 'that is the price.' Peter said to her, 'How could you conspire to test the Spirit of the Lord? Listen! The feet of the men who buried your husband are at the door, and they will carry you out also.' At that moment she fell down at his feet and died. Then the young men came in and, finding her dead, carried her out and buried her beside her husband. Great fear seized the whole church and all who heard about these events."

This story would also appear to depict a word of knowledge given to Peter by the Holy Spirit. We also have the example of the rich young ruler (Matthew 19 verse 16-22) who did not feel able to abandon his riches to follow Jesus. Money is a part of life; we all need it. But let's be ruled by the Holy Spirit, rather being ruled by money!

Jonah

Jonah was given a very specific word by God to go to the city of Nineveh and preach against their great wickedness (Jonah 1:1). Instead of this, he got in a boat and, quite deliberately, headed in completely the opposite direction. Why would he have done this? On first reading the story, you might be forgiven for thinking that he was simply afraid; afraid of having his message rejected, or perhaps even afraid of being persecuted. However, on further reading, we discover that there was something else. After a lot of persuasion, and the use of a large fish (Jonah 1:17-2:10), Jonah eventually obeyed God's Word (Jonah 3:1-4). The Ninevites believed God and repented (Jonah 3:5-10). In fact, we are informed in Jonah 4:11 that there were more than a hundred and twenty thousand people in the city.

Mission accomplished, you would think, and a cause for great relief and celebration on the part of Jonah. If fear had been his motive for running away, then now he could relax, surely? But not a bit of it; Jonah became greatly displeased and angry with the outcome (Jonah 4:1-2). You see, Jonah had a problem of racism. The Israelites and the Ninevites were enemies; Nineveh was the capital of Ashur (Assyria) the biggest enemy of Israel at the time, and Jonah was rather hoping that God would not come to save them! In Jonah 4:3-9 we discover that Jonah appeared to be so full of self-pity and bitterness (after the salvation of the Ninevites) that he considered it better to die than to live. We must learn valuable lessons from this story. First of all, God definitely accepts repentance when it is from a contrite (repenting) heart. Consider 1 Timothy 2:1-6,

> *"I urge, then, first of all, that petitions, prayers, intercession and thanksgiving be made for all people–for kings and all those in authority, that we may live peaceful and quiet lives in all godliness and holiness. This is good, and pleases God our Saviour, who wants all people to be saved and to come to a knowledge of the truth. For there is one God and one mediator between God and mankind, the man Christ Jesus, who gave himself as a ransom for all people."*

God is in the business of saving people, not condemning them. In John 3:16-17 we read,

> *"For God so loved the world that he gave his one and only Son, that whoever believes in him shall not perish but have eternal life. For God did not send his Son into the world to condemn the world, but to save the world through him."*

That is the attitude we must have towards people who are currently not in the Kingdom; God *wants* to save them. Is there any racism within you, however subtle? Coming from England, I know that a lot of my fellow countrymen still have an inherent dislike of German people, despite the fact that the majority of an entire generation have passed away since World War II (it is much better than it was, thankfully). On my travels,

I have observed racism – within the church. When I visited India in 2005, I had the privilege of preaching to some twenty five pastors. There was an interesting reaction to say the least when I mentioned the possibility of God sending some of them to Pakistan as missionaries! Similarly, when I was teaching the Bible to a youth group in Vietnam in 2012, some of them winced at the thought of serving God in neighbouring China! If you have a dislike of a people group for whatever reason – skin colour, historical enmity, etc, then you will never be able to minister the Gospel to them until this is sorted out. Take it to God, repent of it... and perhaps go to that people group to serve them in some way!

Noah

Noah's drunkenness led to the sin of Ham,

> *"Noah, a man of the soil, proceeded to plant a vineyard. When he drank some of its wine, he became drunk and lay uncovered inside his tent. Ham, the father of Canaan, saw his father naked and told his two brothers outside. But Shem and Japheth took a garment and laid it across their shoulders; then they walked in backward and covered their father's naked body. Their faces were turned the other way so that they would not see their father naked. When Noah awoke from his wine and found out what his youngest son had done to him, he said, 'Cursed be Canaan! The lowest of slaves will he be to his brothers.' He also said, 'Praise be to the Lord, the God of Shem! May Canaan be the slave of Shem. May God extend Japheth's territory; may Japheth live in the tents of Shem, and may Canaan be the slave of Japheth.'"*

> (Genesis 9:20-27)

First of all, let's address the issue of alcohol consumption for the Christian. There are many references in the Bible to drunkenness. For example, Ephesians 5:18 says,

> *"Do not get drunk on wine, which leads to debauchery. Instead, be filled with the Spirit."*

(Debauchery is extreme immorality, or excessive indulgence in sensual pleasures). I don't think many Christians disagree on the issue of getting drunk. However, there is strong disagreement on whether it is acceptable for a Christian to drink alcohol at all. Personally, I would point to the fact that Jesus turned water into wine (John 2:1-10) as clear evidence that the drinking of alcohol in itself is not sinful. Also, in Luke 7:34, Jesus, speaking about Himself, said,

> "The Son of Man came eating and drinking, and you say, 'Here is a glutton and a drunkard, a friend of tax collectors and sinners.'"

From that, I would suggest that Jesus declared that He did, indeed, drink alcohol.

Ham

Regarding the sin of Ham, he certainly dishonoured his father in the drunken state in which he found him. Noah subsequently cursed Ham (the father of Canaan), and this curse has survived, many generations later.

Sexual sin

And perhaps this might be a good point to examine the whole area of sexual sin! First of all, Jesus said in Matthew 5:28 that if you even look at a woman lustfully you have already committed adultery with her in your heart. That immediately rules out pornography, then! Pornography has enslaved multitudes of people – including Christians. It is one of the devil's most effective weapons and will, without doubt, prevent you from living life to the full. If you want to be a high-flying goose, then that pornography has to go. You can't do it on your own – you need the Holy Spirit to empower you to be free of it. He in turn – in most cases at least – requires your cooperation. If needs be, switch off the television after 10pm. Go to bed. Ban yourself from going onto those websites where you struggle. Burn those magazines. Do it now; you can return to this book later! Find yourself a trustworthy Christian who you can make yourself accountable to. You are not a victim; God can give you the victory in this area.

Next question, then; how far can I go with a member of the opposite sex (outside of marriage) before I have sinned? As with other issues discussed in this chapter, Christians will disagree. My great friend, the Reverend Emmanuel Ife Babalola from Nigeria, once told me that the Christians in his country laugh at the Christians in the West for even *dating*! They argue that the dating 'game' is very worldly, and that if we were truly living by faith we would not date – split up – date someone else – split up again (possibly a number of times) until we finally end up with the person we want to marry. They consider that the Holy Spirit will *tell* you when you have met the right one; the two of you – if you are walking with God – will both know. He argues that this results in considerably less heartache than western Christians often experience. I can fully respect his view.

Fornication is mentioned quite a few times in the Bible. What does it actually mean? Many believers argue that fornication is any kind of sexual activity outside of marriage, not only the specific sexual act of intercourse. Others say that you can participate in any other kind of sexual activity other than this one specific act, and you are not committing fornication. I certainly would not agree with that. So where do you draw the line? No touching at all? Holding hands? Kissing? Petting? What can you touch, what can't you touch? Well, let's start with 1 Corinthians 6:19-20 where it says,

> *"Do you not know that your bodies are temples of the Holy Spirit, who is in you, whom you have received from God? You are not your own; you were bought at a price. Therefore honour God with your bodies."*

That's an excellent starting point. Ask yourself, "Is what I'm doing honouring to God?" You will know. The Holy Spirit will convict you if you are grieving Him. As John 16:13 says,

> *"He will guide you into all truth."*

Is homosexuality a sin? In today's society, this is a battlefield! Christians who speak out against it are accused of being homophobic, bigoted, intolerant, and so on. No more so than in my native United Kingdom, where there have been some very high profile news stories in the 21st Century. To begin with, there was the case of Peter and Hazel Bull, a Christian couple who ran a bed and breakfast in Cornwall in western England. In 2008, a couple booked a double room in their establishment, and it was only when they turned up that they realised that this was, in fact, a gay couple, Martyn Hall and Steve Preddy. The Bulls had a policy of 'only giving double rooms to married heterosexual couples'. (Note that the house rule they applied was for *any* unmarried couple – it wasn't specifically aimed at homosexuals). As such, they offered Hall and Preddy either a twin room or two single rooms. But Judge Andrew Rutherford ruled the Bulls had discriminated against them on the ground of sexual orientation and awarded them £1,800 each, according to Britain's Equality and Human Rights Commission, which supported the gay couple. My objection to this is: what about the rights of Peter and Hazel Bull to live a Christian life, particularly in their *own home*? Surely if a hotel (or bed and breakfast) advertise themselves as a Christian hotel, then potential guests can then make up their mind if they wish to abide by the house rules or find themselves another hotel?

A second case was in 2012 when Catholic adoption agencies were forced to close down after being informed that they could not refuse to offer children out to gay couples on the grounds of their sexuality. So, once again, rights for homosexuals, but not for people who wish to act upon deeply held religious beliefs. There are plenty of secular adoption agencies who I am sure would be happy to oblige a gay couple if they wished to adopt.

Most recently, the UK government voted in February 2013 to legalise same sex marriage by a margin of 400 votes to 175.

In addition to this, there is an on-going saga in the Church of England as to whether to ordain gay priests, indeed even gay bishops. In the light of all this, we need to ask the question: does the Bible speak about homosexuality? Does it offer scriptures arguing both cases? Here are two that I have found (there are more):

Leviticus 18:22 states,

"Do not have sexual relations with a man as one does with a woman; that is detestable."

Romans 1:18-27 says,

> "The wrath of God is being revealed from heaven against all the godlessness and wickedness of people, who suppress the truth by their wickedness, since what may be known about God is plain to them, because God has made it plain to them. For since the creation of the world God's invisible qualities–his eternal power and divine nature–have been clearly seen, being understood from what has been made, so that people are without excuse. For although they knew God, they neither glorified him as God nor gave thanks to him, but their thinking became futile and their foolish hearts were darkened. Although they claimed to be wise, they became fools and exchanged the glory of the immortal God for images made to look like a mortal human being and birds and animals and reptiles. Therefore God gave them over in the sinful desires of their hearts to sexual impurity for the degrading of their bodies with one another. They exchanged the truth about God for a lie, and worshiped and served created things rather than the Creator–who is forever praised. Amen. Because of this, God gave them over to shameful lusts. Even their women exchanged natural sexual relations for unnatural ones. In the same way the men also abandoned natural relations with women and were inflamed with lust for one another. Men committed shameful acts with other men, and received in themselves the due penalty for their error."

I was unable to find any scriptures in support of homosexuality. For the second time in this chapter, I would ask that you don't shoot the messenger!

Forgiveness

Another area well worth addressing is the whole area of unforgiveness. Are we holding unforgiveness in our heart toward anyone? *If you forgive men when they sin against you, your heavenly Father will forgive you.*

But if you do not forgive men their sins, your Father will not forgive your sins. Strong words from Matthew 6:14-15. Forgiveness is not an 'optional extra'; it is something we are required to do. If we fail to, then it is we ourselves who suffer, rather than the person who has wronged us.

Related to this is the whole issue of past regret. Are you held back by things that happened in the past? Philippians 3:13-14 tells us,

> "But one thing I do: Forgetting what is behind and straining toward what is ahead, I press on toward the goal to win the prize for which God has called me heavenward in Christ Jesus."

This is so important, but of course it is not always easy. Make sure you have forgiven, if that is part of it.

And remember that life is short! Don't waste your emotions fretting on what might have been; it's not worth it. 2 Corinthians 4:16-18 says,

> "Therefore we do not lose heart. Though outwardly we are wasting away, yet inwardly we are being renewed day by day. For our light and momentary troubles are achieving for us an eternal glory that far outweighs them all. So we fix our eyes not on what is seen, but on what is unseen. For what is seen is temporary, but what is unseen is eternal."

That is the bottom line; we won't be here forever. But there is another place where we will be forever. The Gospels speak about the parable of the sower (e.g. Mark 4:1-20). The seed that fell upon the thorns represents a Christian for whom "the worries of this life, the deceitfulness of wealth and the desires for other things come in and choke the word, making it unfruitful" (verse 19). We must guard against this and keep an eternal perspective on life. Psalm 90:10-12 states,

> "The length of our days is seventy years – or eighty, if we have the strength; yet their span is but trouble and sorrow, for they quickly pass, and we fly away. Who knows the power of your anger? For your wrath is as great as the fear that is due you. Teach us to number our days aright, that we may gain a heart of wisdom."

So – ask God to teach you!

The Occult

I think it is also worth addressing the whole area of occult practice. This can be a great stumbling block to faith in Jesus Christ. We are told in Deuteronomy 18:9-12a,

> "When you enter the land the Lord your God is giving you, do not learn to imitate the detestable ways of the nations there. Let no one be found among you who sacrifices their son or daughter in the fire, who practices divination or sorcery, interprets omens, engages in witchcraft, or casts spells, or who is a medium or spiritist or who consults the dead. Anyone who does these things is detestable to the Lord; because of these same detestable practices the Lord your God will drive out those nations before you. You must be blameless before the Lord your God. The nations you will dispossess listen to those who practice sorcery or divination. But as for you, the Lord your God has not permitted you to do so."

I discovered first-hand the reality of a family who had dabbled in occult practice. I went to visit a dear Christian friend of mine, who at that time lived with her parents near London (I won't name this family). The parents were not Christians. The first night I stayed there, I was lying on my bed when I suddenly became aware of the presence of something unpleasant. I tell you the truth, whilst I could not actually see anything, the bed actually depressed near my hip, as if a person were sitting on the bed. I called on the name of Jesus, and the thing – I believe a demon – left me. The following morning I related this story to my friend and she acknowledged that there was a spirit living in that building. The reason? My friend believed because her mother was involved in New Age mysticism, using crystals. Such practice is asking for trouble and gives the enemy a legal foothold into the life of a person. Until such time as her mother would repent of her practice, that spirit was destined to remain.

How much TV are you watching? Maybe a little too much? Use your time productively. TV, of course, can be very interesting and stimulating, but it can also become 'chewing gum for the eyes' if we are not careful. It can also indoctrinate, and bombard us with worldly viewpoints which go against Christian viewpoints. What sort of TV do we watch when we're on our own? What Internet websites do we browse through? I once saw a sign over a fellow Christian's TV: 'Watch what you watch'. A good warning. Guard what goes into your eyes and into your ears.

Let's challenge ourselves with the following:

I HAVE SURRENDERED EVERY AREA OF MY LIFE TO
GOD EXCEPT...........

Victory through weakness
(or "excuses, excuses, excuses")

I once saw the following on my great friend Dave Doyle's fridge (I have expanded it a little):

Do you think you are not able to achieve anything significant for the Kingdom?

Consider the following:

Abraham thought he was too old – he went on to become the father of faith

Jeremiah thought he was too young – he became a great prophet

Joseph was abused – he became a ruler in Egypt

Moses had a speech problem – he delivered the Israelites from captivity

Gideon was afraid – he saved his people from a mighty foreign army

Samson was blind – he won a mighty victory over the Philistines

Rahab was a prostitute – she is now in the genealogical line of Jesus

David was an adulterer and a murderer – he became a great king, also in the line of Jesus

Elijah was suicidal – he became a great prophet

Jonah tried to run away – 120,000 people were saved through him

Naomi was a widow – she led Ruth to Israel. Ruth is also in the line of Jesus

Job had lost his family, was bankrupt and very ill – God restored to him twice what he had started with

Peter denied Jesus – he became a mighty man of God

The disciples fell asleep while praying – they became pioneers of the church

Paul was a multi-murderer who hated the church – one of the greatest Christians of all time

...and Lazarus was dead!!!

So...no more excuses; you're not too married, you're not too single, you're not too busy and you're not too poor. You have massive potential; wherever you are in life, step out and live out your amazing future with God. Technically, the Christian does not need to sin; he chooses to sin. Having said that, I do appreciate that we all have weaknesses. As such, let me comfort you (and myself!) with the following scripture from Hebrews 4:15,

"For we do not have a high priest who is unable to empathize with our weaknesses, but we have one who has been tempted in every way, just as we are–yet he did not sin."

We are not called to work through our weaknesses alone – it is a cooperation with The Almighty.

What happens when disappointment and doubt come?

Lessons from John the Baptist

Disappointment is a part of life; it is unavoidable. What we can influence, however, is our reaction to it. In this section, I would like to focus on a character in the Bible who experienced great disappointment and see how it affected him. There are lessons to be learned. That character was John the Baptist. We begin in the Gospel of Luke, Chapter 1, verses 13-17, where John's birth is foretold to Zechariah, his prospective father,

> "Your wife Elizabeth will bear you a son, and you are to give him the name John. He will be a joy and delight to you, and many will rejoice because of his birth, for he will be great in the sight of the Lord. He is never to take wine or other fermented drink, and he will be filled with the Holy Spirit even from his mother's womb. Many of the people of Israel will he bring back to the Lord their God. And he will go on before the Lord, in the spirit and power of Elijah, to turn the hearts of the fathers to their children and the disobedient to the wisdom of the righteous – to make ready a people prepared for the Lord."

So far so good! It can't be a bad thing to be filled with the Holy Spirit even before the midwife has delivered you! In the sixth month of Elizabeth's pregnancy, Mary now hears that she is to give birth to Jesus (Chapter 1, verses 26-37). We now re-join the story in Luke 1 verses 41-44, where Mary has visited Elizabeth,

> *"When Elizabeth heard Mary's greeting, the baby leapt in her womb, and Elizabeth was filled with the Holy Spirit. In a loud voice she exclaimed: 'Blessed are you among women, and blessed is the child you will bear! But why am I so favoured, that the mother of my Lord should come to me? As soon as the sound of your greeting reached my ears, the baby in my womb leapt for joy.'"*

The Bible tells us in Psalm 42:7 that *Deep calls to deep*. It would seem that this is even possible from within the womb! Now we must fast-forward to John and Jesus in their adulthood. In the Gospel of John Chapter 1, verses 29-34 we read,

> *"The next day John saw Jesus coming toward him and said, 'Look, the Lamb of God, who takes away the sin of the world! This is the one I meant when I said, 'A man who comes after me has surpassed me because he was before me.' I myself did not know him, but the reason I came baptizing with water was that he might be revealed to Israel. Then John gave this testimony: 'I saw the Spirit come down from heaven as a dove and remain on him. I would not have known him, except that the one who sent me to baptize with water told me, 'The man on whom you see the Spirit come down and remain is he who will baptize with the Holy Spirit.' I have seen and testify that this is the son of God."*

God had very clearly and specifically spoken to John, and there was absolutely no doubt in his mind as to who Jesus was. However, at a later date, we read that John challenged King Herod for marrying his brother's wife and was, as a result, imprisoned by the king (refer to Mark 6:14-20). This would, of course, be a huge setback to anybody, and John was no exception. It is clear from scripture that his perspective changed, including his perspective on who Jesus was. In Luke Chapter 7, we read that the fame of Jesus was spreading, culminating in him raising a dead man to life again (verses 11-17). John, from his prison cell, was hearing reports of these things. But he doubted, as we read in verses 18-23,

"John's disciples told him about all these things. Calling two of them, he sent them to the Lord to ask, 'Are you the one who was to come, or should we expect someone else?' When the men came to Jesus, they said, 'John the Baptist sent us to you to ask, "Are you the one to come, or should we expect someone else?"' At that very time, Jesus cured many who had diseases, sicknesses and evil spirits, and gave sight to many who were blind. So he replied to the messengers, 'Go back and report to John what you have seen and heard: The blind receive sight, the lame walk, those who have leprosy are cured, the deaf hear, the dead are raised, and the good news is preached to the poor. Blessed is the man who does not fall away on account of me.'"

What a contrast to John's complete conviction at the time of Jesus' baptism.

And this is our warning; disappointment can lead to a distortion of our perception of reality. John started to doubt. To deal with doubt we must hold to God's revelation about Jesus Christ in spite of our difficult circumstances. Even the greatest men of God are still men of flesh, subject to times of doubt and despair. The mighty prophet Elijah wavered in his faith and ran from the wicked Jezebel, whose prophets he had slain, asking God to take his life. Now, the "Elijah who was to come" wavers as he sits day after day in Herod's prison. Why did John doubt? His prayers and the prayers of his disciples on his behalf to get him out of prison weren't even being answered. John sat in that dark dungeon day after day and may have wondered, "If Jesus is the Messiah, then why am I still in prison?"

Whenever you're going through a time of difficult trials, when it seems that God is ignoring your prayers, be on guard. It was in the context of enduring fiery trials that Peter wrote,

"Be of sober spirit, be on the alert. Your adversary, the devil, prowls about like a roaring lion, seeking someone to devour."

Then he added,

"But resist him, firm in your faith, knowing that the same experiences of suffering are being accomplished by your

*brethren who are in the world. And after you have suffered
for a little while, the God of all grace, who called you to His
eternal glory in Christ, will Himself perfect, confirm, strengthen
and establish you."*

(1 Peter 5:8-10)

Your trials do not mean that God does not exist or that He has lost
control as the Sovereign of the universe. Hang on by faith, knowing that
He will use your trial to strengthen and establish you. As Peter instructs
just a few verses before (5:6-7),

*"Humble yourself under the mighty hand of God ... casting all
your anxiety upon Him, because He cares for you."*

Don't doubt God's sovereignty or His love when you go through
extended trials. Not only was John going through a difficult trial
that would shortly result in his martyrdom, he also was dealing with
disappointed expectations. John was outspoken about God's impending
judgment on sinners. He was bold enough to rebuke even King Herod
for his immorality. But Herod was still having his drunken parties, still
living in immorality with his brother's wife, while John was in prison.
Also, John knew that Isaiah prophesied that Messiah would *"proclaim
freedom to the prisoners and bring in the day of vengeance of our
God"* (Isaiah 61:1, 2). And yet, John wasn't exactly free from prison
and God's vengeance had not been poured out on the likes of Herod.
Besides, the Jews, especially the religious leaders, weren't flocking to
submit to Jesus as their Messiah. So John's expectations about Jesus
were disappointed.

Maybe you've been there, too? You thought that Jesus would solve
all sorts of problems for you, but instead, the problems have grown
worse. You thought that He would make life easier and more abundant,
but it has been more difficult and destitute. Perhaps some well meaning
adviser came along and told you that the reason things weren't going
so well is that you weren't praying enough. So you prayed more, but
the problems persisted. Then you confessed every sin you could think
of, and prayed some more, but God still didn't seem to be listening. It's
easy for even the godly to doubt at such times.

So what's the answer? Holding to God's revelation concerning Jesus Christ is vital in difficult times. We need to remember that Jesus will come twice-the first time to baptize with the Holy Spirit; the second time to baptize with the fire of judgment as He will bring the vengeance of our God (Isaiah. 61:1-2; Luke 4:18-21). When as a believer you're struggling with doubt, take your doubts to Jesus in prayer. Make sure your heart is in submission to Him. Pour out your confusion or difficulty to the Lord. Reading solid, Bible-believing commentators may help you clarify a matter, and so this can help. But in all your study, you need to lay hold of Jesus Himself. So bring your doubts to Him; go back to the basic question, Who is Jesus Christ? Read the Gospels. Could He have been a con man? Or do His life and teaching ring true? In John 6, Jesus taught some difficult things and as a result, many who had been following Him withdrew. Jesus asked the twelve,

"You do not want to go away also, do you?"

Peter gave the great reply,

"Lord, to whom shall we go? You have words of eternal life. And we have believed and have come to know that You are the Holy One of God."

(John 6:68-69)

When you struggle with doubt, look to the person and work of Jesus Christ Himself. Where else can I go? I know that Jesus is who He claimed to be. He is the promised Messiah. He is the only Saviour. He is risen from the dead. I may not understand everything, but if I cling to Jesus, I will come through the storms of doubt into calmer seas. Look to God's revelation about His Son and hold to it in spite of your difficult circumstances. Lord I believe; help my unbelief!

God's guidance through trials

Lessons from Joseph

God is sovereign and He is in control. It may not always feel that way. It may not have seemed that way to the next character we will study, but as we see the beginning from the perspective of the end, we discover that God was guiding Joseph's life the whole way through.

The story begins in Genesis 37, with Joseph at the age of seventeen. Loved more by his father (Jacob) than were the other sons, they hated him. It was perhaps inadvisable, therefore, for him to proclaim so boldly two dreams he received (clearly from God, it later transpired) in which they were bowing down before him. Was he oblivious to their hatred? Was he boasting? Possibly he was, or maybe we can put his approach down to the impetuosity of youth. Either way, this was the final straw for his jealous brothers, and they took their opportunity to first of all throw him into an empty cistern and later sell him to some Ishmaelites who took him to Egypt.

Was God guiding his life? It certainly did not appear so at that point. But He really was. Joseph's example to us was exemplary; we have much to learn from him. Throughout all the trials he went through (that we have seen thus far and will see as we develop this story), not once do we read of him developing a root of bitterness or resentment in any shape or form. He remained faithful to God, and God prospered him, despite setbacks along the way, which God was fully aware of and had allowed for. We take up the story in Genesis Chapter 39, verses 2-6,

"The Lord was with Joseph and he prospered, and he lived in the house of his Egyptian master. When his master saw that the Lord was with him and that the Lord gave him success in

everything he did, Joseph found favour in his eyes and became
his attendant. Potiphar [his master] put him in charge of his
household, and he entrusted to his care everything he owned.
From the time he put him in charge of his household and of all
that he owned, the Lord blessed the household of the Egyptian
because of Joseph. The blessing of the Lord was on everything
Potiphar had, both in the house and in the field. So he left in
Joseph's care everything he had; with Joseph in charge, he did
not concern himself with anything except the food he ate."

This should be a model for us in our work situations! I certainly pray
that it is in mine. So things were going well for Joseph until Potiphar's
wife took a bit of a fancy to him. Through her lies, he found himself in
prison, accused of sexual harassment. But even in prison, God's blessing
continued to be showered upon Joseph, as is recorded in verses 21-23,

"But while Joseph was there in the prison, the Lord was with
him; he showed him kindness and granted him favour in the
eyes of the prison warden. So the warden put Joseph in charge
of all those held in the prison, and he was made responsible
for all that was done there. The warden paid no attention
to anything under Joseph's care, because the Lord was with
Joseph and gave him success in whatever he did."

In prison, Joseph was able, through divine intervention, to accurately
interpret the dreams of two inmates (Chapter 40). Joseph believed that
this would provide him with a ticket out of there, but he was quickly
forgotten by the inmate he saw released, and remained there a further
two years. Another opportunity for Joseph to abandon his faith and
decide that there was no God that loved and cared for him. Would
you have done so in Joseph's position? And surely this was conclusive
proof that God was not, in fact, guiding Joseph's life? But no; Joseph
kept his heart pure towards God and God kept His considerable hand
upon Joseph.

Joseph's release came about when Pharaoh also had dreams and
Joseph was required to interpret them, which he did with precision
through God's enabling (Chapter 41). There were to be seven years

of abundance in the land, followed by seven years of famine. Joseph even recommended the course of action that should be followed – to store enough food during the years of abundance to compensate for the famine. Subsequently, Joseph was entrusted with this task and was put in charge of the whole land of Egypt (Genesis 41:41). Joseph was now thirty years old; God had guided him thus far, through a variety of trials. The same is true for you and me. Under Joseph's stewardship, Egypt prospered greatly, whilst all the nations around them became impoverished. From Genesis Chapter 42, we begin to see the fulfilment of Joseph's own dreams – his family bowing down before him. Joseph was presented with his opportunity for revenge. He didn't take it. In fact, we read of a man who had clearly forgiven the evil done against him. He even fully acknowledged God's guiding hand, in Genesis 50:20, by declaring,

> "You intended to harm me, but God intended it for good to accomplish what is now being done, the saving of many lives."

God intended it. Nothing happened by chance. There was no 'Plan B'. God was sovereign all along, totally in control. We need to take a leaf out of Joseph's book and react in similar fashion when all kinds of trials come our way. We don't live in a perfect world and things don't always go to (our!) plan. Let's turn to the Book of James (Chapter 1:2-4) to discover a godly attitude to trials,

> "Consider it pure joy, my brothers, whenever you face trials of many kinds, because you know that the testing of your faith develops perseverance. Perseverance must finish its work so that you may be mature and complete, not lacking anything."

So it's pure joy, then! The message is: keep going. Don't give up, no matter how tough it gets. Stay in the Word, keep communicating with God, preferably not with a bitter heart. Stay in fellowship with other Christians. Have an attitude of worship, or an 'attitude of gratitude' as I've heard on a few occasions. The apostle Paul offers us good advice in Philippians 4:4-7 when he says,

"Rejoice in the Lord always. I will say it again: Rejoice! Let your gentleness be evident to all. The Lord is near. Do not be anxious about anything, but in everything, by prayer and petition, with thanksgiving, present your requests to God. And the peace of God, which transcends all understanding, will guard your hearts and minds in Christ Jesus."

I have leaned on this passage of scripture on countless occasions, to such an extent that I have even committed it to memory. However, you might argue that it is unrealistic – even impossible – to fully obey this instruction. Rejoice *always*? Can that really be done? Even through times of great grief? My dad passed away in December 2010, which was a time of great sadness for me and my family, especially Mum, of course. How can we "rejoice" when something like that has just happened? It is a difficult one to address, I have to confess, but I do have one or two ideas on this. First of all, we need to recognise that there is a difference between 'joy' and 'happiness'. Joy is a fruit of the Spirit, as found in Galatians Chapter 5, along with love, peace, patience, kindness, goodness, faithfulness, gentleness and self-control. These are things which are – or should be – *constants* in the life of a Christian. And don't forget we are called to rejoice *in the Lord* always rather than in the circumstances. Nehemiah 8:10 tells us that *"the joy of the Lord is your strength"*. It is in these times of grief that God's joy can sustain us, despite the absence of happiness during such a period. Happiness is not a constant – it will depend on what is going on in our lives – although it is true that different people have different capacities to be happy. In connection with this, we do need to recognise that just as there are seasons (Spring, Summer, Autumn, Winter) in the natural, there are also 'seasons' in our individual lives as Ecclesiastes Chapter 3 tells us,

"There is a time for everything, and a season for every activity under the heavens: a time to be born and a time to die, a time to plant and a time to uproot, a time to kill and a time to heal, a time to tear down and a time to build, a time to weep and a time to laugh, a time to mourn and a time to dance, a time to scatter stones and a time to gather them, a time to embrace and a time to refrain from embracing, a time to search and

a time to give up, a time to keep and a time to throw away, a time to tear and a time to mend, a time to be silent and a time to speak, a time to love and a time to hate, a time for war and a time for peace."

Suffering is an integral part of life and it is critical that we adopt a godly, mature attitude when suffering comes our way, as it inevitably will. Incidentally, the seasons don't necessarily need to follow in the same order; there is no reason why Autumn can't be followed by Summer again!

Let's examine the life of a spiritual giant (David) and see how he reacted to various 'seasons' in his life.

"Blessed are those you choose and bring near to live in your courts! We are filled with the good things of your house, of your holy temple."

"You care for the land and water it; you enrich it abundantly. The streams of God are filled with water to provide the people with grain, for so you have ordained it. You drench its furrows and level its ridges; you soften it with showers and bless its crops. You crown the year with your bounty, and your carts overflow with abundance. The grasslands of the wilderness overflow; the hills are clothed with gladness. The meadows are covered with flocks and the valleys are mantled with grain; they shout for joy and sing."

(Psalm 65:4 and 9-13)

This is Summer time in David's life (in this case, quite literally as well as metaphorically). Things are going abundantly well for him. Verse 1 tells us how he reacts to it,

"Praise awaits you, our God, in Zion; to you our vows will be fulfilled."

"As the deer pants for streams of water, so my soul pants for you, my God. My soul thirsts for God, for the living God. When

can I go and meet with God? My tears have been my food day and night while people say to me all day long, "Where is your God?"

(Psalm 42:1-3)

So, a much tougher time in David's life. How had things been previously? Well, we are told in verse 4,

"These things I remember as I pour out my soul: how I used to go to the house of God under the protection of the Mighty One with shouts of joy and praise among the festive throng."

Things had previously been wonderful for him, so arguably he's moved to an 'Autumn' period in his life. So how does he react to it? Verse 5 tells us,

"Why, my soul, are you downcast? Why so disturbed within me? Put your hope in God, for I will yet praise him, my Saviour and my God."

Yes – he actually gives his soul an instruction! He is going to trust God as well as praise Him.

Psalm 22:1-18,

"My God, my God, why have you forsaken me? Why are you so far from saving me, so far from my cries of anguish? My God, I cry out by day, but you do not answer, by night, but I find no rest. Yet you are enthroned as the Holy One; you are the one Israel praises. In you our ancestors put their trust; they trusted and you delivered them. To you they cried out and were saved; in you they trusted and were not put to shame. But I am a worm and not a man, scorned by everyone, despised by the people. All who see me mock me; they hurl insults, shaking their heads. 'He trusts in the Lord,' they say, 'let the Lord rescue him. Let him deliver him, since he delights in him.' Yet you brought me out of the womb; you made me trust in you, even at my mother's breast. From birth I was cast on you; from

my mother's womb you have been my God. Do not be far from me, for trouble is near and there is no one to help. Many bulls surround me; strong bulls of Bashan encircle me. Roaring lions that tear their prey open their mouths wide against me. I am poured out like water, and all my bones are out of joint. My heart has turned to wax; it has melted within me. My mouth is dried up like a potsherd, and my tongue sticks to the roof of my mouth; you lay me in the dust of death. Dogs surround me, a pack of villains encircles me; they pierce my hands and my feet. All my bones are on display; people stare and gloat over me. They divide my clothes among them and cast lots for my garment."

This is Winter time in David's life. Things are dire. And at the same time, what an incredible prophetic word for a crucifixion which was still hundreds of years into the future. How does he react to it? We find out in verses 19-31,

"But you, Lord, do not be far from me. You are my strength; come quickly to help me. Deliver me from the sword, my precious life from the power of the dogs. Rescue me from the mouth of the lions; save me from the horns of the wild oxen. I will declare your name to my people; in the assembly I will praise you. You who fear the Lord, praise him! All you descendants of Jacob, honour him! Revere him, all you descendants of Israel! For he has not despised or scorned the suffering of the afflicted one; he has not hidden his face from him but has listened to his cry for help. From you comes the theme of my praise in the great assembly; before those who fear you I will fulfil my vows. The poor will eat and be satisfied; those who seek the Lord will praise him – may your hearts live forever! All the ends of the earth will remember and turn to the Lord, and all the families of the nations will bow down before him, for dominion belongs to the Lord and he rules over the nations. All the rich of the earth will feast and worship; all who go down to the dust will kneel before him – those who cannot keep themselves alive. Posterity will serve him; future generations will be told about

the Lord. They will proclaim his righteousness, declaring to a
people yet unborn: He has done it!."

He called out to God and trusted Him for the future; that things would
turn out well with God at the helm.

"[He] set my feet upon a rock, making my steps secure. He put
a new song in my mouth, a song of praise to our God. Many
will see and fear, and put their trust in the Lord."

(Psalm 40:2-3)

How had things been previously? Verse 2 tells us,

"He drew me up from the pit of destruction, out of the
miry bog."

This is Spring time in David's life. Things had been grim, but they have
now turned the corner and there is a new optimism.

How does he react to it? Verses 3-10 tell us,

"Many will see and fear the Lord and put their trust in him.
Blessed is the one who trusts in the Lord who does not look to
the proud, to those who turn aside to false gods. Many, O Lord
my God, are the wonders you have done, the things you planned
for us. None can compare with you; were I to speak and tell of
your deeds, they would be too many to declare. Sacrifice and
offering you did not desire–but my ears you have opened–burnt
offerings and sin offerings you did not require. Then I said, 'Here
I am, I have come–it is written about me in the scroll. I desire to
do your will, my God; your law is within my heart.' I proclaim your
saving acts in the great assembly; I do not seal my lips, Lord, as
you know. I do not hide your righteousness in my heart; I speak
of your faithfulness and your saving help. I do not conceal your
love and your faithfulness from the great assembly."

In short, he is going to continue to trust God but – more than that – he
is going to tell others of God's goodness to him.

PART 3

Final thoughts

The Great Commission or the Great Omission?

What are you living for? What is the purpose of your life? What motivates you when you get out of bed in the morning? We all (or most of us) have goals. What are your goals? Perhaps you want to be the best father or mother you can possibly be to your children. Maybe you want to be that wonderful husband or wife. Your desire might to be to fulfil your career potential, which in turn will enable you to provide well for others. Some people wish to travel extensively during their lifetime. There might be projects you wish to get involved with. These are all highly commendable goals. But now read the following,

> *"Then Jesus came to them and said, 'All authority in heaven and on earth has been given to me. Therefore go and make disciples of all nations, baptizing them in the name of the Father and of the Son and of the Holy Spirit, and teaching them to obey everything I have commanded you. And surely I am with you always, to the very end of the age.'"*
>
> (Matthew 28:18-20)

These were Jesus' last words to His disciples before He ascended into Heaven. It is known as "The Great Commission". How do these words affect you? Do they spur you to action? Or do you read them with indifference? Look again at your plans, your goals, your dreams. Are they Kingdom of God-centred? I am so challenged by Matthew 28:18-20. What greater goal could I have in life? What is going to really count at the end of the day?, the 'end of the day' ultimately being Judgement Day, of course. I am comforted by the fact that Jesus has saved me.

"For it is by grace you have been saved, through faith–and this is not from yourselves, it is the gift of God–not by works, so that no one can boast."

(Ephesians 2:8-9)

Nonetheless, we still have a mandate and I don't want to be seriously embarrassed at the end of my life when I am kneeling before Almighty God. I want to hear God say, "Well done."

All of the goals outlined in the first paragraph of this chapter can, I would suggest, still apply. But perhaps they need to fall into line with an overriding goal to play your part in the Great Commission? Teach your children the right things. Encourage your wife or husband in the things of God. Use your career success to help fund Gospel-related projects. Travel extensively, taking the love and Good News of God with you. You don't need to abandon your goals! Just recognise that we have a higher calling which these can fit in with. As you read the following passage of scripture, you will see that these people failed to do this,

"When one of those at the table with him heard this, he said to Jesus, 'Blessed is the one who will eat at the feast in the kingdom of God.' Jesus replied: A certain man was preparing a great banquet and invited many guests. At the time of the banquet he sent his servant to tell those who had been invited, 'Come, for everything is now ready.' But they all alike began to make excuses. The first said, 'I have just bought a field, and I must go and see it. Please excuse me.' Another said, 'I have just bought five yoke of oxen, and I'm on my way to try them out. Please excuse me.' Still another said, 'I just got married, so I can't come.' The servant came back and reported this to his master. Then the owner of the house became angry and ordered his servant, 'Go out quickly into the streets and alleys of the town and bring in the poor, the crippled, the blind and the lame.' 'Sir,' the servant said, 'what you ordered has been done, but there is still room.' Then the master told his servant, 'Go out to the roads and country lanes and compel them to come in, so that my house will be full. I tell you, not one of those who were invited will get a taste of my banquet.'"

(Luke 14:15-24)

So let's ask one or two searching questions: Is it wrong to buy a field? No. Is it wrong to buy five yoke of oxen? No. Is it wrong to get married? No. And yet the master became angry. Why? Because the people in question had put these things in place of serving him, rather than bringing them into line with serving him. We must be so careful not to make the same mistake with the things which occupy our attention.

Discovering your calling

So what role does God want you to play? How can you decide what your particular ministry will be within the Body of Christ? Well, what are your natural giftings? Are you good with children? Or youth? Are you a natural teacher? Are you a leader or a supporter? Are you practical? Are you good at administration? Are you good at handling money? Are you good at languages? That might be a good starting point. I always remember a previous pastor of mine, Andy Elmes from Portsmouth, relating his conversion (I think around about 1990). He describes himself at that moment as "a lump of clay"! He had no idea what lay ahead for him, but one thing he did say to God was "I've got a big mouth and a big imagination"! Guess what? Today he is an inspirational preacher and a tremendous visionary. As I write, he has planted eight churches around Hampshire, England, and is planning to plant one, possibly two a year over the next few years, perhaps for as long as he has strength to do so.

In my case, I am a natural teacher. My main paid work since the early to mid 1990s has been the teaching of English as a foreign language. As such, I also feel very comfortable when it comes to teaching the Bible (of course you have to know your subject!). It is something I enjoy doing. In addition, I relate very well to children, and children's ministry has always come very naturally to me. And at this point, I would like to relate to you a story of how God spoke to me regarding my calling.

I became a Christian in 1985. In 1988 I joined a church – Chichester Christian Fellowship (Bognor Regis congregation) – and was asked if I would like to help with the children's ministry. This I did (and greatly enjoyed) until I moved to Jamaica in 1991. Apart from some children's work on outreach in Trinidad, that was my last children's work (within a church setting) for a number of years. It simply lay dormant through circumstances such as two years in Spain followed by periods in churches where there were no (or at least very small) children's ministries on account of the ages of the congregations!

Fast forward a few years, and I was enjoying a Christian holiday known as Spring Harvest in Minehead, England. Lying on my bed, I was praying when I suddenly saw (in the Spirit) some traffic lights. What was unusual about these traffic lights was that they were painted yellow, which British traffic lights are not. In my mind I was thinking, "Does God want me to travel again? If so, where?" I began to imagine countries which might have yellow-painted traffic lights. Anyway, later that day (or was it the following day?) I was walking through the Spring Harvest campus when what should I see? You've guessed it – some yellow-painted traffic lights! They were not real traffic lights, but artificial ones, not quite as high as me! The significant thing though, was what they were there for; they were outside – and part of – the children's ministry of Spring Harvest! God was calling me to get involved with children's ministry once again! So I did!

You will have your own unique set of giftings. Start there, and let God take you on an exciting journey!

How big is your God?

God od wants to guide your life. I believe that by having a greater concept of the magnitude of God, we will have a greater understanding of what God is capable of DOING. If we have a greater understanding of what God is capable of doing, then I believe we will take more risks – more steps of faith; we will have greater expectations of greater miracles than we had previously been believing for. We will be invincible!

Let's start with a basic concept: we believe that God created the world. Let's turn to Hebrews 11.3,

> *"By faith we understand that the universe was formed at God's command, so that what is seen was not made out of what was visible."*

Now let's turn to Romans 1.20,

> *"For since the creation of the world, God's invisible qualities – His eternal Power and divine nature – have been clearly seen, being understood from what has been made, so that men are without excuse."*

So...we believe that God created the universe and we have no excuse but to believe it!

Our Earth seems huge to us, with its massive continents, oceans, mountains etc. But when we consider our place in God's creation, suddenly, we're not so big! There are planets much bigger than ours in the Solar System. Remember – God created all these! He is greater! But it doesn't stop there! If we bring The Sun into the equation, we become very, very, small indeed! Don't forget...God also created the Sun! And we mustn't forget that this is only the Solar

System...God's creation extends much, much, further than this! GOD IS MASSIVE!

So...if God created all this by His Word, can you imagine what fantastic things He is capable of doing on our very very small Earth?! And in our miniscule lives, for that matter! Please try to imagine, because this is important. I believe that in our minds and in our hearts we have made God very small. We need a greater perspective of God. Let's examine a few scriptures to remind ourselves of the greatness of God,

> "Who has measured the waters in the hollow of His hand, or with the breadth of His hand marked off the Heavens? Who has held the dust of the Earth in a basket, or weighed the mountains on the scales and the hills in a balance? Who has understood the mind of the Lord, or instructed Him as His counselor? Whom did the Lord consult to enlighten Him, and who taught Him the right way? Who was it that taught Him knowledge or showed Him the path of understanding? Surely the nations are like a drop in a bucket; they are regarded as dust on the scales; He weighs the islands as though they were fine dust."
>
> (Isaiah 40.12-15)

I also recommend that you read Job Chapters 38 and 39, where God challenges us to consider what He has made. And, thus, His greatness.

Has it become clearer? God is bigger than we have made Him. We need to change our perspective!

We are the Body of Christ; Jesus is the Head. In the natural world, the body is held together by a substance known as laminin. Without laminin, the body would collapse. Incredibly, the structure of laminin resembles a crucifix! In the spiritual realm, Jesus is the laminin! He holds His body (the church) together. He holds the universe together! If you don't believe me, let's turn to Colossians 1.17,

> "He is before all things, and in Him all things hold together. And He is the head of the body, the church."

I recommend that you watch a video of the American preacher Louie Giglio, on the subject of laminin. It is truly remarkable.

Jesus said in John 14.12,

"You will do greater things than me."

Do we believe this? Imagine doing greater things than Jesus did! Do we really believe it...in our hearts? We need to step out in faith much much more than we do at the moment. We need to expel demons with greater regularity. We need to place our hands on the sick with greater regularity. We need to be asking for the impossible with greater regularity.

Step out of your comfort zone

The Lord is your shepherd, absolutely. But shepherding implies that the sheep need to move! You need to allow yourself to be shepherded. Lying in bed all day every day won't result in you having a very exciting life! The Lord was Noah's shepherd, but Noah was required to build. The Lord was Abram's shepherd, but Abram was required to set off on his travels. As was I. God gave me visions of Jamaica, Sweden, Brazil, India and Vietnam, but I still had to get myself to these places! The Christian walk is essentially the believer cooperating with God; God provides the ability, but we must provide the availability. When we read the final part of the Gospel of Mark, after Jesus has given the Great Commission, we see in Chapter 16:20,

> *"Then the disciples went out and preached everywhere, and the Lord worked with them and confirmed His word by the signs that accompanied it."*

Faith is active. In James 2:18 we read,

> *"Show me your faith without deeds, and I will show you my faith by what I do."*

We are not saved *by* good works, but we are certainly saved *to* good works. What are your dreams? Do you have big dreams? What can you do to reach those dreams? In the world of psychology, there are three situations or "zones". One is called "The Comfort Zone". Things are OK, they're comfortable. Maybe you're a believer, maybe you're part of a church. But – life is monotonous; you're not taking any risks! You're not expecting God to do incredible things in your life. You are not believing in miracles. At the other extreme, there is a zone called "The Panic

Zone" where you are living in constant stress, perhaps without the Holy Spirit. What we really need is a balance between these which is called "The Stretch Zone" where we are stepping out and we are growing. We are taking a few chances. Have you found your ministry in the church? If not – keep looking! Is it time for you to start laying hands on the sick? Have you tried preaching? Can you teach the Bible? Could you become more evangelistic? Can you learn another language? Can you be part of a church plant? Can you be part of the children's team? Have a good stretch! Take a few risks! Do a few crazy things!

Why Jesus Christ?

If I were to answer this question fully, I would need to write another book! However, I will make a few observations, because this was a stumbling block for me back in the 1980s when I was searching for truth. Now – many years on – I have a transformed life as well as the many experiences I have related in this book to enable me to know that Jesus is "The One", so to speak. I don't need any more convincing.

But let's look also at the amazing claims of Jesus Christ,

"I Am the Light of the world. He who follows Me shall not walk in darkness, but have the light of Life."

(John 8:12)

"I Am the Way, the Truth and the Life. No one comes to the Father except through Me."

(John 14:6)

"I Am the Resurrection and the Life. He who believes in Me, though he may die, he shall live. And whoever lives and believes in Me shall never die."

(John 11:25-26)

"I Am the Good Shepherd. The Good Shepherd gives His life for the sheep."

(John 10:11)

"I Am the Bread of Life. He who comes to Me shall never hunger, and he who believes in Me shall never thirst."

(John 6:35)

"I Am the Door. If anyone enters by Me, he will be saved."

(John 10:9)

The above are not the words of someone who was merely a 'good man'. To paraphrase C. S. Lewis in his book "Mere Christianity", to make such claims about yourself, you are either a liar, a lunatic or, in fact, you are telling the truth – in which case you are Lord. Personally, I go for the latter of these, but you must make your own mind up.

Taking a first step?

I hope you have enjoyed reading my book and have got something out of it. Before I close, I would like to extend an invitation to those of you who have not yet received Jesus Christ as your Lord and Saviour. Find yourself a quiet place and say words similar to the following:

> *"Lord Jesus Christ, I believe that you are the Son of God and Saviour of the world. I recognise that I have messed up (I am a sinner). I have done many things that don't please you. I have lived my life for myself. I am sorry and I repent. I ask you to forgive me. I believe that you died on the cross for me, to save me. You did what I could not do for myself. I come to you now and ask you to come into my life and take control of my life, I give it to you. Help me to live every day in a way that pleases you. I love you, Lord, and I thank you that I will spend all eternity with you.*
> *Amen."*

It's not a set formula, so use your own language to communicate how you feel. I did something similar a number of years ago, and it was the best decision I ever made; my life was transformed from that moment on. If you prayed the above prayer from the heart, then you now have Jesus Christ. In fact, He will be living within you. The Bible tells us this in Colossians 1.27,

> *Christ in you, the hope of glory.*

So, bless you, and I wish you well on your life's journey!

Steve